Praise for *Aligned Abundance*

"A fascinating, original and helpful book for anyone seriously interested in making their ethical ambitions real."
Robin Sharma, #1 worldwide bestselling author of *The 5AM Club* and *The Monk Who Sold His Ferrari*

"Emma Mumford's tools really work and will get you the manifestation results you want."
Mel Robbins, author of *New York Times* bestseller *The 5 Second Rule*

"*Aligned Abundance* is a must-read for anyone seeking to harness the power of manifestation in a way that feels authentic and achievable. Emma Mumford has created a guide that inspires and empowers."
Amy Leigh Mercree, medical intuitive and bestselling author of 19 books, including *Aura Alchemy* and *The Atomic Element Healing Oracle*

"If you're ready to align with your highest potential and attract the life you deserve, this book is the perfect companion."
Emma Howarth, author of *A Year of Mystical Thinking* and an astrologer at *Glamour*

"An insightful, practical guide to unlocking your true abundance potential."
Poppy Delbridge, leading expert in tapping and energy work, and the bestselling author of *Tapping In*.

"This book will set you on the path to shaping the life you've always dreamed of."
Radhika Das, mantra artist, author and host of For Soul's Sake podcast

"If you're ready to stop chasing and start receiving, *Aligned Abundance* is the key you've been waiting for! Emma's grounded approach shows you how to attract abundance by aligning with your true self, not by forcing outcomes. Her teachings cut through common manifesting myths, empowering you to create real, lasting change from within."

George Lizos, bestselling author of *Ancient Manifestation Secrets* **and** *Protect Your Light*

"Emma Mumford's Aligned Abundance feels like having a Life Path 33 mentor by your side—because that's exactly what she is. A manifesting expert and wise old soul, Emma makes the journey to abundance practical, relatable, and inspiring. She takes the overwhelming world of abundance and makes it practical, relatable, and genuinely inspiring. If you're ready to turn your dreams into reality, Emma's got you covered"

Kaitlyn Kaerhart, bestselling author of *You Are Cosmic Code: Essential Numerology*

EMMA MUMFORD

ALIGNED

Abundance

Release expectations,
become magnetic
and manifest the life
of your dreams

WATKINS

Aligned Abundance
Emma Mumford

First published in the UK and USA in 2025 by
Watkins, an imprint of Watkins Media Limited
Unit 11, Shepperton House, 83–89 Shepperton Road
London N1 3DF

enquiries@watkinspublishing.com, www.watkinspublishing.com

Publisher: Fiona Robertson
Project Editor: Brittany Willis
Head of Design: Karen Smith
Illustrations: Alice Claire Coleman

A CIP record for this book is available from the British Library

ISBN: 978-1-78678-952-5 (Paperback)
ISBN: 978-1-78678-958-7 (eBook)

MIX
Paper | Supporting
responsible forestry
FSC
www.fsc.org   FSC® C171272

10 9 8 7 6 5 4 3 2 1

Typeset by Lapiz
Printed and bound by CPI Group (UK) Ltd, Croydon, CR0 4YY

The manufacturer's authorised representative in the EU for
product safety is: **eucomply OÜ** - Pärnu mnt 139b-14, 11317
Tallinn, Estonia, hello@eucompliancepartner.com,
www.eucompliancepartner.com

For Alex, Luna and Grandad Malcolm.

Alignment is a journey, not a destination.
I dedicate this book to those who are seeking a reset,
shift or magic in their life and to those seeking
a breakthrough. May alignment and the deepest
of joys find you and enrich your life.

Contents

Introduction

Alignment has become a heavily used word in the manifestation (aka Law of Attraction) space, yet many people still don't know much about it or what alignment really means in manifesting. In fact, over the last nine years of my manifesting journey, some of the most common questions I've been asked include:

- "I feel out of alignment – what do I do?"
- "How can I align with my desire?"
- "What does alignment actually mean?"

We'll be exploring the answers to these sorts of questions together in this book. After taking you on a deep inner-work journey with my last book, *Hurt, Healing, Healed*, I wanted to (1) write a lighter and more joyful book, and (2) write a book that would give you the next steps in your journey, looking at the deeper questions about manifesting and what happens once you've done the inner work. Now, hopefully you'll know from reading my previous books that the inner work is an ongoing journey throughout our life here on Earth, and funnily enough alignment follows suit. Alignment is a journey, not a destination, and I deeply feel the alignment process with yourself and your desires happens after the "believe" or inner-work step of your manifestation journey (see page 7). Don't worry, though, if you haven't read my previous books or any other manifestation books for that matter, you can still enjoy and benefit from *Aligned Abundance* as we're going to start right at the beginning.

So what led me to writing a book on alignment? According to a Forbes business article, only 8 per cent of the world's population manage to turn their dreams into reality. It's a statistic that is often quoted in other studies, but whether or not it's true, it seems that billions of people on this planet die with their dreams still in them – this is a HUGE number of dreams and manifestations that are sadly never lived. Researching these studies shocked me, as given the rise in awareness around manifesting in recent years, it feels like every person and their dog now knows about manifesting because of the internet, great books being released about the subject and TikTok. The word "manifest" was even named the word of the year by Cambridge Dictionary with an impressive 130,000 searches on their website in 2024. Google searches for the term "manifesting" spiked in 2020 by 600 per cent according to *Elle* India and have only continued to grow in momentum. On TikTok, the hashtag #manifesting now has over 25 billion views. Seeing these incredible figures feels magical, as back in 2016, when I first came across the Law of Attraction, manifestation and spirituality were still very much thought of as taboo and "woo woo" subjects.

How does all this tie in with alignment? I believe the problem why so many people struggle with manifesting their desires is because they're manifesting from a place of overwhelmed, stressed and ungrounded energy; whereas alignment means manifesting from a place of balance and being an energetic match for whatever it is that you want to attract. Now, this isn't anyone's fault; old school teachings tell us to go "all in" and, also, life just happens – we can't all be Zen and love and light every single day. But most importantly, the Law of Attraction is hugely misunderstood and if you're not in alignment with your authentic self and your desires, then sorry to break it to you: your desire isn't going to manifest anytime soon!

The good news is that, although all these stats may seem heavy and you may even relate to feeling overwhelmed with manifesting or frustrated that, no matter what you do, it doesn't seem to work for you, don't worry; I've got you. I've created this very book to answer your questions on why manifesting has felt hard and why you've seen inconsistent results so far.

So if you feel like you've been doing ALL the work and you're still not seeing results, rest assured that *Aligned Abundance* isn't about keeping you stuck in a cycle of healing, constant work and being reliant on my work or anybody else's. This book is about integration, self-empowerment, embodiment, up-levelling and magnetizing. While there are tools and practices in this book, they aren't designed to create more work for you; they're only there to help you embody the lessons and see the results of the manifestation work you've already done. This book is about doing less, receiving more and aligning; there will be no hustle, no making you feel like you have endless work to do, or that you can't have fun in the process of manifesting your dreams. It gets to be easy, it gets to be fun and it gets to feel effortless!

What Exactly is Alignment?

The term "alignment" first started to be linked to the manifestation process in around the early 2000s with books such as *The Secret* by Rhonda Byrne, in which she touches upon aligning your thoughts, feelings and energy with your desires in order to manifest them. However, we can go even further back, to the late 1930s, when Napoleon Hill referred to the power of harmony leading to success and abundance in his book *Think and Grow Rich*. Although these teachings didn't use the term "alignment" in the exact same way it's used today, it's clear to see that, while the term isn't new, our understanding of how manifestation and energy work has come on in leaps and bounds.

Simply put, alignment means that your energy, your vibration and your desires are aligned with each other. It's a bit like the concept of manifestation, in that your decisions, energy, beliefs and habits all create a frequency that aligns you with a certain reality – whether that's your desired reality or not.

I like to describe alignment as being like a radio station: you've got the car radio switched on and an annoying song starts to play, so you switch station and – boom! – your favourite song starts playing; you feel instantly lifted and before you know it, you're happy, singing along and on your way. You know that real banger of a song that you know all the words to? It's the same thing with our desires: we have the power to change our vibration and frequency to tune in to the energy (i.e., radio station) of our manifestations and abundance. Although many believe that they have to become a whole new person in the manifestation process to manifest their desire, that simply isn't true. The good news is that you're already the version of yourself who's attracting your desire: you just need to change the station (by adapting your own frequency) to tune in to the right channel for your desired reality.

What is Aligned Abundance?

To me, aligned abundance means abundance that feels effortless, brings you peace and manifests with ease. It's abundance that's grounded in your values and self-worth, and that elevates and uplifts your life. It's the type of abundance that runs deeper than superficial manifesting. It's not about the "stuff" you want; instead, it's about deeply aligned feelings and experiences. The journey of manifesting aligned abundance reconnects you with yourself, helps you turn your magnetism back up and, most importantly, it feels safe to your body, because you've already done all the necessary inner work.

It's your own version of abundance in which you're rooted in your why, but also in how your abundance can positively impact the collective, too. Aligned abundance is about those desires that are rooted in your truth (your inner knowing), the highest good and the soul moments that are destined to happen in your life. It's the abundance that takes you by surprise, it's the warm glow of the sun on your skin and those times where your heart feels total and utter bliss in the moment. That, my gorgeous friends, is aligned abundance.

Now, that's my spiritual way of explaining alignment, but in a more grounded way, we often hear people say, "It's not in alignment with me," whether they're spiritual or not. I've even seen the term used on one of the popular real estate shows on Netflix, where they were talking about "aligned buyers". Essentially, we've been using the term "alignment" for a long time now to define what our "yes" and "no" are, and what brings us joy around the small and the big decisions we take in life – whether that's deciding whether to go to brunch with your friends, or even which country to live in. Today, the word "alignment" is used in so many ways, but it's time to understand it on a deeper level and how it can help us to elevate our frequency and the quality of our experiences – which is what this book is all about.

My Journey with Alignment

So what qualifies me to write this book for you? I've dedicated over the last three years of my life and work to deeply understanding, thoroughly researching and even embodying alignment through many of my teachings and offerings, so that I can share these tools with you. As I went through my own personal journey with alignment, I would often joke with my good friend George that once again "These lessons are going to make a great book one day!" and I wasn't wrong. I know the score now with the Universe: that I'm going to live and breathe a book before I write it. It now feels like the right time to share this special book with you, in the hopes that it too changes your life and allows you to manifest your dreams in an aligned and easy way.

In a professional capacity, I'm an award-winning manifesting coach and three-times-bestselling author, Law of Attraction YouTuber, speaker and host of the #1 spirituality podcast on iTunes "Spiritual Queen's Badass Podcast". My work helps people turn their dream life into an abundant reality using the Law of Attraction and spirituality. It's my mission and purpose to help you clear the blocks to abundance and live a Positively Wealthy life full of your wildest dreams. I've been an entrepreneur for over 13 years and have been doing this specific work for over nine years now. During this last decade, my work has helped hundreds of thousands of people around the world to manifest incredible abundance in their lives!

On a personal level, funnily enough alignment has been part of the journey I've lived and breathed in all my books over the last few years. After I finished writing *Hurt, Healing, Healed* in early 2022, I made huge breakthroughs with my healing journey and my manifesting practice has only deepened as a result. I've found the subject of alignment come up time and time again in all areas of my life, in my client sessions, on my Instagram Q&As and even at in-person events; after sharing with my community that my word for 2022 was "Alignment", the alignment journey and questions on alignment haven't stopped for me since.

In 2022, when this idea for this, my fourth book, dropped into my head, I did some research and to my surprise found there were absolutely zero books on alignment! None, and when I thought about it, I realized I'd learned my own alignment practice over the years through manifesting my desires and through my own teachings deepening. I hadn't read about alignment in a book; I hadn't seen anything anywhere else that explained how important alignment is in the manifesting process and how actually working on alignment is such a powerful tool that, in my experience, can bring your desires into your life *very* quickly!

My aim in this book is to highlight the importance of alignment in the manifesting process and how alignment is actually the key to changing your whole incredible life! If I could give just one tip that would hugely change someone's life when it comes to manifesting with ease it would be: "Work on your alignment and all of your heart's desires will follow."

Manifesting doesn't have to be hard, yet I feel old-school teachings and even vague short clips on TikTok, for example, just aren't getting to the real nitty gritty or core essence of manifesting. My goal with this book is to remind you that manifesting gets to be easy, manifesting is for everyone, and that manifesting from a regulated and grounded state will change your life forever. This is the book for you when you feel off-kilter, the book to help you reset, pivot and finally align with your desires. *Aligned Abundance* will be your loving guide to unravelling what you've learned about manifesting so far in order to help you keep what works and declutter what doesn't feel in alignment for you anymore. It will help you to get clear on what you really do want and offer you practical yet powerful ways to attract aligned abundance into your life.

Throughout this book, I will take you deep into the alignment process that I embarked on back in 2022 when creating my bestselling course "Attract, Alignment, Abundance". Not only is that entire course about manifesting and alignment, but launching the course and having record-breaking numbers of people sign up for it blew every expectation of mine out of the water and showed me exactly how these alignment teachings work in all areas of our life – and how needed this work and book are. This course confirmed so much for me in terms of my alignment teachings and while it's helped to shape this book, my own alignment journey has continued to deepen since deciding to write it.

During the first week of the course, I get the people who sign up for this inner work – who I call Spiritual Queens, or Queens for short, as members of my community – to unlock their authentic self, and I explain how this is the first step in our alignment process. At this stage, I often get comments from course members saying: "But Emma, I don't know who my authentic self is, so how can I align with them?" and that's where our journey together will begin. So don't panic if you don't yet know all the answers; it's my job to lovingly guide you through the alignment process and to help you unlock your true magnetism to be able to manifest with ease in a new and exciting way.

By the end of our *Aligned Abundance* journey, you'll have amped up your magnetism to all kinds of abundance in your life. In reading this book:

- You'll discover how alignment fits into the manifestation process and identify where in your life you may be feeling out of alignment, and unlock shifts and miracles in these areas.
- You'll be able to identify when you feel out of alignment and reclaim your power to align with positive new identities that help you embody your desired reality.
- You'll turn up your magnetism and be able to manifest abundance from a regulated nervous system in easy and effortless ways.
- You'll learn how decluttering your energy can make space for aligned abundance.
- You'll release control and expectations around your manifestations and be equipped with an extensive toolkit to help you develop and manifest from a place of unwavering trust in the Universe.
- You'll unlock the power of flow, which will enable aligned abundance to stream into your life.
- You'll become aligned with your inner and outer seasons and you'll become in tune with the cyclical nature of alignment in your life.

At the end of each chapter, you'll find key practices and journaling prompts to help you embody the teachings in it. To get the most out of these, you may want to dedicate a special notebook or journal to your *Aligned Abundance* journey. You will also find a set of "Aligned Reflections" that sum up the key teachings in the chapter.

I would recommend going through Part One in order, as the steps and practices have been mapped out in a certain way to help you release, reset and realign. However, Part Two can be read and actioned in any order, so trust where you feel called to go. Take this book at your own pace: alignment can't be rushed and you'll know when it's time to move on to another chapter or action. Trust in the divine wisdom within you as well as my guidance throughout the book.

In addition to the section of useful resources at the end of this book (see pages 225–8), you can access more resources, meditations and other extras on my website: www.emmamumford.co.uk/alignedabundance

Set Your Aligned Abundance Intention

Before we dive into all of the goodness within these pages, I want to invite you to think about what called you to pick it up in the first place. What alignment are you seeking?

As you'll discover, intention is everything, so as you begin your journey I want you to set an intention for what you'd like to manifest, experience or feel by the time you've finished reading *Aligned Abundance*. Think about where you'd like to be and how you'd like to feel. Or maybe you picked up this book to see progress or shifts with your manifestations? If so, mention that. In your chosen notebook or journal write down what your intention/manifestation is for your journey with this book. Make sure it feels magnetic, expansive and exciting. To get you started, here are some examples for how you can word your aligned abundance intention:

- By the end of *Aligned Abundance*, I'll be crystal-clear on my next move.
- By the end of the book, I will feel magnetic, joyful and in alignment.
- I have released the blocks to my desires and am now experiencing my dream relationship.
- I have manifested £10,000 through the path of least resistance and in a way that felt easy and effortless.
- My body is happy, healthy and thriving.
- I am a magnet to abundance; the reality I desire is here now.

Once you've set your powerful intention, write it down in your journal, sit back and grab a cup of your favourite drink, and we'll begin.

As you'll discover, the aligned abundance journey is full of fun and excitement, so get ready to cultivate joy, fun and most importantly alignment! Please do let me know how you get on as you go through the book, as I'd love to hear your aligned abundance stories. Keep me updated on your journey and what alignment manifests for you as a result of doing this work. If you'd like to be a part of our fantastic community and have accountability during your journey with this book, you can join my free "Law of Attraction Support Group" on Facebook, where you can connect with myself and other like-minded souls as we talk about all things manifesting and spirituality! It's a beautiful group of people from all over the world, so come on over and join us as we'd all love to support and cheerlead you along this powerful journey.

Are you ready to align with your higher self and manifest your wildest dreams? Hell, YASS you are, so let's get started ...

#AlignedAbundance
@iamemmamumford | www.emmamumford.co.uk

PART ONE

Discover Alignment

"Aligning your life is a never-ending process. It is a day-by-day, moment-to-moment practice. Not a one-off overhaul. Living a life of alignment is a daily practice. Checking in, staying on course, redirecting as you travel. Noticing what feels good, free, and spacious, and what feels restrictive, stagnant, and stuck. What is falling away and what is ready to rise."

Rebecca Campbell, author and spiritual teacher

In Part One, we will explore together how our alignment impacts our manifestations, how we become out of alignment and how alignment shows up in our day-to-day life. I'll gently guide you through my alignment process and how you can start to embody alignment in all areas of your life.

By the end of Part One, you'll be aware of your alignment blocks and what's keeping you stuck, and you'll be feeling much more in alignment, regulated and rooted, and connected to your higher self. You'll also be ready to effortlessly magnetize abundance and aware of your highest timeline – this is a path or reality where your actions, thoughts and choices are in alignment with your highest self. It's often described as a state of greater ease, flow and fulfilment as you align with your core values and the universal energy of expansion and growth.

The Law of Attraction and Alignment

As we begin our alignment journey together, I want to dive deeper into what alignment is in the manifestation process and how this can help us remove the blocks to our magnetism and effortlessly align with our desired reality. Manifestation itself is as easy as breathing – but we're the ones who create resistance, who block our magnetism and who project expectations onto our beautiful desires. As your alignment guide, I want to take you first of all into the basics of manifestation and alignment, and why this work is so important.

My Five Steps to Manifestation

Essentially, the Law of Attraction is the belief that we can attract anything into our lives. It's one of the seven energetic laws of the Universe and it's all about having a positive and grateful mindset. It's about being conscious that if we can see something in our mind, we can hold it in our hands. Like attracts like.

"A bit like karma" is the best way I can explain the Law of Attraction. What you put out into the world you get back. For example, if you're putting out positive, happy and grateful energy, you're going to attract lots of incredible miracles into your life, including more positivity. There are no limits to what you can manifest – you can manifest materialistic abundance such as money, your dream career, your dream home and other possessions. You can also manifest emotional abundance such as healing, happiness, joy, your dream relationship and love. However, if you're being negative, expecting the worst to happen and doubting everything, then guess what? Your life isn't going to look too great.

The Law of Attraction also teaches us that our words, thoughts and vibration are creating our reality – so wherever your energy goes, it will manifest into your reality. The Universe matches our energy, so essentially we get what we accept in life. Traditionally, in books and teachings, the Law of Attraction has three steps: ask, believe, receive. While I feel these steps are absolutely necessary, I very quickly found that they weren't deep or thorough enough for my personal manifestation journey. The jump between steps two and three felt huge to me and like the process was missing many of the valuable insights in unlocking abundance that I'd discovered in my own life. So, when I was writing my first manifestation book back in 2018, I sat down and considered all that I had learned so far, and I channelled five powerful steps that now feature in all my work. Many people tell me how much more sense these steps make and how the Law of Attraction feels more attainable when following them.

1. Ask

The first and most important step is to ask the Universe, God, Source, Divine – whatever it is you resonate with – for your desire. It's really important to know exactly what you want and to be specific, as the Universe is like a divine mirror and your level of clarity will be reflected back to you. Don't worry if you have absolutely no idea right now what it is you want in life; the Universe will soon help you out along the way. I always find that focusing on things that bring me joy is a great way to establish what I want. You don't just have to manifest materialistic things; you can manifest emotions, answers and guidance galore! You can even manifest to be shown what your next step should be. The way to ask the Universe can be as simple as saying it out loud – for example, "Universe, I would like to manifest my monthly salary increasing." I always like to add, "And so it is" at the end in order to see it as done. Whether you keep a goals list, say your manifestation verbally, write it down as an affirmation, think it or put it on a vision board, this is ALL asking, and you only need to ask once.

2. Believe

The second step is to believe that your desire can and will manifest. Now, I know some of you will be saying, "Well, I've asked. So how come my money, dream career and love of my life aren't knocking at my door yet?!" The answer is alignment: the Universe is responding to your current energy, identities and beliefs. Everything will manifest at exactly the right time for your highest good. If you find it hard to believe that your desire can be yours, then ask the Universe for a sign. Connect to your angels, spirit guides or simply the Universe, and ask for a sign that your desire has been heard. Once you've set your intention you may notice some resistance comes up for you, or even that your inner critic/ego pipes up with negative or doubting thoughts. Take a look at your inner world to see if there are any limiting beliefs, fears or blocks standing in the way of you and your desire. Explore any blocks that do come up and work to release them.

3. Trust

This important step is one that I've added to the manifestation process. It may sound similar to "believe", but the two are quite separate. There will be a period when you're waiting for your manifestation to appear. Manifestation is a co-creation process with the Universe so, in this step, you need to meet the Universe halfway with inspired and aligned action. Essentially, this means acting as if you already have your desire. For example, if you want to manifest your dream partner, you would take yourself on dates, commit to yourself, take inspired action and love yourself. After all, if you had your dream partner you would be relaxed, feeling loved and getting on with your life. You wouldn't be sitting indoors waiting on a text or being miserable. So, really connect to the feelings you would experience if your heart's desire were here right now, and embody them fully! Think about what action you need to take to put yourself in the field of opportunity and possibility with your desire – for example, updating your CV or résumé, or planning what outfit to wear for an important event so you can dress to impress.

4. Let Go

Arguably one of the most important steps in the Law of Attraction, this is another one that I've added. Although letting go is vital to the manifestation process, for some reason most Law of Attraction methods skip past it. So, let it all go! It seems confusing that you should ask for your desire and then forget all about it, right? Crazy, I know, but it actually makes things happen so much faster. Letting go means that you're totally okay with either outcome. If you want or need something so badly that you become desperate about it, you risk putting out a vibration of lack, so that's what you will attract more of: lack. Believing your desire will manifest, while at the same time being really grateful for what you have now and accepting the possibility of a different outcome, is an absolute game changer. This is the miracle: seeing how far you have come, honouring your growth and not even needing the manifestation anymore. You still hold that manifestation as your end goal, but you release how and when it will happen. By doing this, you will attract your desire more quickly; and by living in the now, having fun and focusing on other things, you let the Universe get to work!

5. Receive

This is the final step: receiving your manifestation. Receiving is still a part of the process, so really challenge yourself to get into the energy of receiving – how much do you allow yourself to receive in all areas of your life? It's a time to celebrate, so let the partying begin! You may receive signs, numbers or even snippets of intuition that your manifestation is on the way. I often sense something the day before it happens. If you do, just relax and let yourself be excited! And when your manifestation does materialize, honour your journey, thank the Universe and express gratitude for this wonderful abundance.

＊ ＊ ＊

You may be wondering where exactly alignment sits in the manifestation process. Although alignment is mainly embodied in the third and fourth steps, it can actually be found in all five of them. Being in alignment allows you to set aligned intentions that feel good from the get-go in step one; it helps you to identify any potential blocks or resistance in step two; it enables you to take aligned action in step three, and then to embody the version of yourself who has your desire in step four; and, finally, it plays a key part in receiving your aligned abundance in the fifth step.

Although my alignment practices and the tools featured in this book can help you in whatever stage of the manifestation process you're currently in, you'll find you naturally place more focus on alignment during the shift in energy that happens in the third and fourth steps. As you take aligned action in the third step to meet the Universe halfway, you'll then start to take an energetic step back and allow the Universe to deliver your desire. While you're letting go in the fourth step what you're really doing is "acting as if" or embodying the version of yourself who has your desire. You're aligning the identities, beliefs and habits of this version of yourself that you've worked on in the three prior steps to magnetize this desire into your reality by literally becoming the energetic match to your desire.

Embodiment is Key

Okay, maybe you've come across some of these ideas before, yet despite everything, you still feel stuck? Many people comment how, after reading self-help books, they feel like they're caught up in a constant cycle of self-improvement. Reading more and more books and doing more courses only makes them feel like a constant work in progress – never reaching the holy grail of "healed" or "perfect". Although I believe we continue to learn and up-level throughout our entire life, I agree that many of us can get stuck in a cycle of self-improvement, relying on book after book to provide that magical fix.

While my books and others like them provide incredible tools, inspiration and words of wisdom, there is one thing I see time and time again that people miss in this process: embodiment. The reason why people feel like they've done all the work but their inner world is still not reflected in the outer world, is because they're not embodying the healing work they've done so far.

The key to manifestation is embodying your desire. We first bring in desire through spirit, then into the mind (cognitive) and then into the body (physical). And in order to embody our desire, we have to be in alignment with it. To revisit that earlier analogy of mine, it's a bit like tuning in the car radio properly, instead of listening to the crackling static of the airways.

I also like to use the following analogy to explain what too much self-help work can do: imagine if you were taking lots of different supplements, how could you possibly know which one had worked? In the same way, if you're doing multiple self-help healing modalities, how will you know if anything's worked if you keep on adding more? This is why after therapy or healing sessions the practitioner will very often tell you not to do any more sessions for a few days, or even for up to a week afterwards, to give your subconscious and self time to process and integrate. Embodiment is an important piece of the puzzle, which we'll be exploring in more detail in chapter 13, where I'll introduce you to an amazing manifestation technique based on it.

For now, please let me remind you that you're not a constant work in progress; you're a beautiful masterpiece who – with the guidance in these pages – is going to be aligning all the parts within and without yourself, to create a beautiful environment for yourself and your life. If you feel like you need to put all those self-help books down, put them down! Take a break and pick them up again when you feel called to and, if not, enjoy some fiction or immerse yourself in experiencing the life you've already worked so hard to create. This is alignment: listening to yourself, your intuition and knowing when it's a season of picking up books and being active, versus enjoying life and integrating the lessons you've learned so far.

The Two Pillars of Manifestation Alignment

Over my years of working with alignment, I've come to the realization that two key steps are part of the process. I want to share these with you now, as they're echoed throughout the pages of this book and in the "Aligned Actions" you'll find at the end of each chapter. They shaped how I created my "Attract, Alignment, Abundance" course (which sparked the idea for this book, back in 2022).

Pillar #1: Alignment within Yourself

Coming into alignment with your external world requires you to come into alignment within yourself first. This can look like:

- aligning within your mind, body and spirit
- reconnecting
- grounding back in
- discovering and expressing your authentic self
- strengthening your intuition
- honouring your body

- making aligned decisions – decisions that match your own values
- knowing when to walk away from what's no longer serving you and keeping you stuck

Pillar #2: Alignment with your Desire

Once you're experiencing alignment internally, this can now be reflected into the outer world through flow, abundance and aligning with the version of yourself who is a match for your desire. This can look like:

- flowing over forcing
- embodying the emotions and feelings of your desired outcome
- becoming the version of yourself who has your desire through embodiment practices that will help magnetize your new reality to you
- taking aligned and inspired action to meet the Universe halfway
- surrendering to the divine plan for your life

Three Types of Alignment

There are also three types of alignment we can experience in our life, which are separate to the two pillars of manifestation alignment. Understanding this can help you to dive deeper into what alignment looks like in your life right now, how to start listening to what's in alignment and how to make empowered aligned decisions.

Daily Alignment

This form of micro alignment focuses on the choices and decisions we make daily to bring joy and purpose into our routine. Maybe your workout has felt uninspiring recently, or staying home instead of travelling this summer has made you feel all kinds of out of alignment? Daily alignment concerns these sorts of relatively minor decisions, which can change frequently and which we make every day to enhance our wellbeing and vibration. These micro daily alignments create the core and foundation for the overall feeling of alignment in our life.

Seasonal Alignment

This is all about the season of life you're currently in. It may represent the outer physical season (like spring, for example), but it can often be the metaphysical seasons we experience within ourselves. These decisions impact our life on a larger scale, such as our purpose in that moment in time, where we live, our friendship circle, work, finances and home. These seasonally aligned actions and decisions often impact us over the coming months or years, and will change from season to season.

Soul Alignment

This type of alignment is about the grand scheme for your life and the collective. For example, I know this book is in soul alignment with my higher self and purpose, but I've been tested around it, as it hasn't always felt in alignment to write each week. However, I still know this book is needed and that my writer's block will be temporary (I actually believe that writer's block is a form of alignment block), so it's not something I need to put down and which will never see the light of day. Whereas seasonal and daily alignment are more micro-focused and ever-changing, I see soul alignment as concerning our major life decisions, like studying for that master's degree even if you've no idea whether you'll get your dream job afterwards; who you choose to spend your life with; whether or not to have children; or where to live and what your purpose and gifts are, such as writing books or working with charities. These are soul desires that we'll feel a deep sense of alignment with, and while these can change and evolve over time, they feel more rooted and long term.

* * *

The secret to working with these three types of alignment is knowing that by focusing on the micro daily alignments, these will start to add up to seasonal and soul alignment. It all begins with you and your day-to-day decisions and aligned actions. You'll know what to do and your aligned actions will happen as if by magic. You can start to help yourself by making empowered decisions.

Empowered Decisions and Aligned Action

Alignment is about empowerment, and taking aligned action means making empowered decisions that align with yourself. When it comes to making these decisions, the Universe will never punish you for exploring all your options and being informed about them. After all, how will you know what aligned action is with your current situation if you're basing your decisions on blind faith alone?

For example, if you're worried about exploring IVF, debt management, medication or any other worst-case scenario because you think your miracle won't manifest in this area of your life, then don't be. You only need to decide on your next best step; many miracle manifestation babies are born via IVF and I've even heard of stories where the IVF didn't work and the couple end up conceiving naturally against all odds, or manifested a family in another way! Accepting help or the facts of your current situation will never stop the miracles flowing to you. You don't need to know how the miracle will appear or how your manifestation will come into fruition; you only need know the next best step that feels in alignment to you. This is how alignment is created: through moment-to-moment choices that bring you closer to your desires. When faced with seemingly impossible decisions, a great question to ask yourself is, "Is this bringing me closer to my desired outcome or further away?"

If you're someone who can sit there fully grounded in the knowledge that the perfect creative solution will come for your manifestation, great – then trust that. However, I know from my own experiences that I'd feel anxious and worried, which wouldn't manifest the result I wanted. By exploring the options and if needs be, facing your worst-case scenario, you help take the fear away and can make aligned empowered decisions that feel in alignment to you there and then.

Others' Alignment

I can already hear you saying, "Well, this is great, Emma, but my [insert: loved one, family member or friend] isn't on board with my aligned decisions!" Another part of the alignment process is the gentle acceptance that your version of alignment may not look like other people's version. The great part about alignment is that it will look different for everyone and we should always respect and honour this.

If a decision or choice is really in alignment for you, then the Universe will align its manifestation for you – for example, partners will agree out of nowhere that it's a great idea or they may even agree first time! Somehow and in some way, your aligned abundance will happen. Alignment is about operating from your truth and listening to your intuition, surrendering this to the Universe and allowing what is for the highest good of everyone collectively to emerge. Maybe your partner rejecting the house that you were desperate to buy means an even more aligned and more incredible house can come forward! And don't confuse your alignment with control, as whatever is meant for you will never pass you by.

When Things Seem Out of Alignment

The alignment process is all about switching your energy, beliefs and frequency to match the desired outcome where your wildest dreams will manifest! Along the way, you may have some doubts about whether you're on the right track, so let's look at this now.

Your Manifestations Aren't Meant to Feel Safe

Sometimes we can even feel out of alignment when setting intentions, whether that's because the goal isn't really aligned with our core values and dreams, or we feel the pressure to manifest what others are manifesting. In some cases, it comes down to a fear of declaring what it is that we truly want. This is why some people can struggle to get direction or clarity on their desires: because of the fear of naming what it is they really want, or fear of judgement around this, or the fear of doing what it will take to manifest that desire. If you're playing small out of fear, your soul will be letting you know about it – and maybe even reading this paragraph is making you think, "Wow, Emma's hit the nail on the head."

While your desires should feel physically safe and good for you in general, in the beginning they're meant to scare you a little. (I'll be going to go into this in more detail in chapter 4, "Manifest from a Place of Regulation".) Nothing beneficial ever came from staying in your comfort zone, and the same goes for manifestation. Your goals aren't meant to feel safe, normal or easy at first, otherwise – guess what? You'd already have them here, in your world! Your goals are glimpses into who you can become and they're an initiation. They're meant to up-level you and challenge you to become a whole new version of yourself, the version of you who is aligned with that desire or goal and has it in their life. So if they scare you – good! It's my job to gently take your hand and help you believe they're possible, closer than you think and feel as easy as breathing to your subconscious mind.

Resistance

I see resistance as being slightly different to mental blocks and limiting beliefs: resistance feels more action-based rather than solely mindset-focused. While resistance to our desires can absolutely be down to a deep-rooted limiting belief or fear, it can show up in many areas of our life. However, I see it most commonly in the third step of my manifesting process – "Trust" – when it's time to take aligned and inspired action. For example, if you're resisting fixing that warning light on the car, getting a check-up at the dentist or doing your tax return, you can guarantee that abundance will be resisting you too!

It really did shock me how much my life shifted when I stopped resisting going to the dentist and got over my fear. It took me years to bite the bullet and get the necessary fillings done, and afterwards, I honestly couldn't even tell you what the fear underneath it all had been. I felt such relief when I met my lovely new dentist, who put me right at ease. After I started regularly looking after my teeth, having check-ups and getting the necessary work done, my money blocks in my business magically disappeared!

While we are all guilty of putting things off and avoiding the things we know we need to do, avoiding these things is actually sending out signals to the Universe of resistance and blocks. This is why, when looking at your own resistance to taking action, you need to look at what else you're resisting in your life. You may really want that perfect job to manifest, for example, but if you're resisting putting yourself out there, where else are you stopping the flow of abundance?

The quickest way to create flow in your life once again is to deal with all the mundane things you've been resisting and clear them off your to-do list. You'll feel a weight lift off your mind and have clear, flowing energy to focus on your desires. I often find the action I need to take comes through so clearly once I've dealt with my resistance, as I then have the mental space and time in my life to give it my full attention and energy.

Your job is turn up your magnetism, not to start repelling things; avoidance and resistance are two of the main causes for your magnetism to become blocked and stagnant. So I want to challenge you today to start thinking about what you're resisting in life: what feels stuck, stagnant or blocked when it comes to your desires?

I've Manifested Something I Don't Want!

We've all been there – when we've manifested something huge in our life and further down the line, we realize that actually we don't want that manifestation anymore. Then we may start to question why we manifested something we didn't really want in the first place, and what the purpose of this was.

The good news is you can always leave the job, relationship or whatever it is that hasn't worked out – and, yes, there was a reason for it to manifest. The Universe is simply showing you alignment in action: it's showing you what you were in alignment with at that moment in time, and how you're destined for more. The Universe will never give you peace in a situation you weren't meant to settle in.

Just because you are manifesting, this doesn't mean you're exempt from life, soul contracts or up-levelling. If you've asked for a certain desire to be fulfilled, maybe that very manifestation was meant to highlight where you're still playing small and how you were never meant to settle for that version of abundance. The situation may not be what you wanted, but it's what you needed so that you can get clarity around what you *really do want* and what you won't settle in. By aligning within yourself first, grounding into your desires and setting aligned intentions from the get-go, you'll no longer find yourself wondering why you've manifested something that you now realize you don't really want, because you'll be too busy experiencing the opposite and enjoying the aligned soul abundance in your reality. This is why I created this book and the aligned abundance principles: you don't need to manifest any "tests" from the Universe that ask you to rethink your dreams if you're manifesting from a place of alignment!

MY ALIGNMENT PROTOCOL

As you progress through this book, you'll begin to fine-tune your intuition of whether things are in or out of alignment in your life. If you're feeling blocked or stuck, or have manifested something that you no longer want, then you might be right to suspect that things aren't in alignment for you. If that's the case, there are three simple steps that you can take:

1. **Stop:** If it was aligned, it would be flowing. If a manifestation, project or even relationship feels like an uphill struggle, doors keep closing and you're experiencing endless frustration no matter how much work you do, it's time to stop and reassess your alignment with this situation.
2. **Reset:** If something is feeling out of alignment, it's time to reset the energy, as old ways won't open new doors. How can you reset the energy of this situation energetically and with your actions?
3. **Realign:** How can you reframe this situation? What is the opportunity being presented here from the Universe? Reframe the situation and use this as an opportunity to come into alignment with yourself, your priorities and move forward from a new state of alignment and flow.

We Always Align Forward, not Backward

Even though it can feel like it, we never go backward in life and, in the same way, we always align forward. I often get messages from my wonderful community, saying they feel like they've taken 10 steps back; that they don't feel in alignment and that old fears are rearing their heads again. The fact is that time isn't linear, it's cyclical, but while we revisit these cycles, we are never at the same frequency as before – we're revisiting this from a different energetic frequency.

The past is gone and the future never comes; we only ever have a series of present moments. So if you feel like you aren't making progress, what you're really experiencing is stagnation or resistance in the present moment. You're never moving backward, only ever up-levelling, aligning and magnetizing in the present moment. Another great reminder is that we can only ever receive our desires in the present moment, so if that's not the perfect permission slip to get present I don't know what is!

But what do I mean when I say we're revisiting the present moment from a different energetic frequency? Your vibration, energy and frequency play a key role in manifesting and living in a state of aligned abundance, which is why we're going to be taking a closer look at this next. I can't wait to guide you through the process of alignment and help you experience aligned abundance in all areas of your life!

Aligned Actions

Action

For your first aligned action in this book, I want you to reflect on your previous manifestations or, if you haven't manifested before, on a situation in your life when you received your goal but it turned out to be something you didn't want after all. Journal or reflect on what this manifestation or experience taught you. What clarity or alignment came out of manifesting something you didn't want?

Intention

Reflect on this chapter and think about where you may be doing too many healing practices without embodying the manifestation work you've already done. Challenge yourself to strip back any practices or tools that feel stuck or stagnant, and think about how you can start to do less and raise your vibration (see chapter 2). If you're doing lots of daily practices that are keeping you stuck in the 'Ask' step, such as affirmations, visualization, intention-setting, scripting and meditation all for one desire, then challenge yourself to stop asking, as you only need to ask for your desire once, and start moving along the five-step process described on pages 6–8.

Journaling Prompts

- What does alignment mean to me?
- What does alignment look like in this season of my life?

- What feels stuck, stagnant or blocked when it comes to my desires?
- What am I resisting or avoiding in my life?
- What did I learn when I manifested something I didn't want?
- What empowered decisions do I feel called to make?
- What aligned action can I start to lean into?

ALIGNED REFLECTIONS

- Manifestation is as easy as breathing: we're the ones who create resistance, who block our own magnetism and who project expectations onto our beautiful desires.
- The journey of manifesting aligned abundance reconnects you with yourself, helps you turn your magnetism back up and, most importantly, it feels safe to your body because you've done the inner work.
- Your goals aren't meant to feel safe, normal or easy at first – otherwise, guess what? You'd already have them here in your world!
- If you're resisting fixing that warning light on the car, getting a check-up at the dentist or doing your tax return, you can guarantee that abundance will be resisting you too!
- The Universe will never give you peace in a situation you weren't meant to settle in.
- You never really move backward; you are only ever up-levelling, aligning and magnetizing in the present moment.
- By exploring the options and facing your worst-case scenario, you take the fear away and can make aligned empowered decisions that feel in alignment to you there and then.
- You're not a constant work in progress, you're a beautiful masterpiece aligning all the parts to create a beautiful environment within yourself and life.
- Your version of alignment may not look like how other people think it should.
- Whatever is meant for you will never pass you by.

Raise Your Vibration

Although the subtitle of this book suggests I'm going to teach you how to become magnetic to your desires – and don't worry, I still am! – the good news is that you're already magnetic. Nothing can switch off your magnetism or ability to manifest. It's simply time to amp it up and effortlessly align with the abundance waiting for you. To start this process, I want us to begin with the foundations of energy and frequency and to start to turn up your magnetism.

The key to creating consistency with your manifestation and alignment practice is through intention, devotion and raising your vibration. I'm often asked how to stay motivated with manifesting and the answer is creating a devotional, intentional practice you enjoy. When we have fun we raise our vibration and this in turn creates emotional and vibrational consistency, which reflects into our outer world as consistent habits, abundance or flow. Our vibration and energy play a big role in our alignment journey and, just like alignment, our vibration is cyclical too. The two go hand in hand, which is why working on your vibration is the key starting point to creating consistency and turning up your magnetism to align with the incredible abundance waiting for you.

However, without some solid foundations in place, you'll find both your energy and alignment will rollercoaster, with no grounding middle point. The aim of the game is to create consistency with both your alignment and vibration so you always have a solid centre to return to in any season of your life.

What is Your Vibration?

Your vibration is the energetic frequency or state of being that you radiate. Everything in this Universe, including humans, is thought to vibrate at different frequencies. These frequencies are influenced by our thoughts, emotions and actions. Higher vibrations are associated with positive emotions such as love, compassion, joy and peace, while lower vibrations are linked to fear, anger, jealousy and other negative feelings. The Law of Attraction states that like attracts like: high vibrations therefore attract positive experiences, people and opportunities, while lower vibrations can mirror negativity.

Now, an important reminder here is that we don't live in a world of instantaneous manifestation, so not every negative thought or emotion will manifest into your life. We have on average between 60,000 to 80,000 thoughts a day and, no, not all of them manifest (thankfully); but what does manifest is your consistent vibration, identities and beliefs. Your vibration represents your energetic essence and by consciously elevating your vibration, you align more with your authentic self, your higher self and the divine flow of the Universe.

Here are some ways we experience vibration daily:

Energy frequency: As mentioned, everything from physical objects to thoughts are believed to have a vibrational frequency. Higher frequencies are lighter, more harmonious and closer to spiritual enlightenment, while lower frequencies feel denser and cause duality and a disconnection with self.

Emotional impact: Our emotions significantly impact our vibration. Positive emotions like gratitude or joy raise our frequency, while negative emotions like guilt or despair lower it. As we know from the Law of Attraction, like attracts like, which is why you must create a consistent state of vibrational (and emotional) harmony to experience the emotions and reality you desire to experience.

Higher self: As we go along our spiritual journey and expand our awareness, our connection to our higher self, the Universe and our vibrational consistency will increase. This can look like heightened intuition, deeper compassion and a stronger connection to the Universe and your spirit team (see page 35).

How to Raise Your Vibration

So how do we get into a feeling of alignment when we're in a space of low vibration? I was recently interviewed by a lovely lady called Victoria, and we talked about alignment in the manifestation process. She asked me, "How do we manifest from the space we're in and get to the point where we're an energetic match for our desire, if we've been doing all the things we should?" Here's what I shared on her podcast …

Build Consistency

You have to meet yourself where you're at and the season of life you're in currently. We can't be high vibe 24/7; not even I am! Honouring your energy and emotions is important if you want to build a steady and solid base level of vibration. The bad days teach us what happy days feel like and vice versa: we only know what joy feels like from experiencing sadness. This is the Law of Polarity in action (another of the seven energetic laws that I talk a lot about in my work).

Raising your vibration isn't done through faking it until you make it; that route can lead to you experiencing extreme highs and extreme lows, a bit like a rollercoaster ride. Instead, it's through creating a daily practice that supports you, honouring your emotions and exploring these, and finding tools that support you and uplift you. All of this will help you create emotional regulation, which in turn creates a stable vibration. This means that even when you experience the inevitable highs and lows of life, your emotional state will stay grounded and regulated, and you'll be able to feel higher vibrations more quickly, consistently and authentically.

Raising your vibration means clearing any blocks or resistance to experiencing higher vibrations, so whether you choose to do this through journaling, therapy, EFT (tapping), affirmations, breathwork, yoga, dancing, connecting to nature, inner work or listening to high-vibrational music, to name a few options, building consistency and finding the right tools to support you is the first place to start. I also find it helpful to think about the emotional guidance scale.

The emotional scale: I first learned about the power of our vibration and emotions through reading Esther and Jerry Hicks's book *Ask and It Is Given*. In it, they share their channelled emotional guidance scale and how we can continually move up and down this scale. The aim of this scale is not to suggest there are any bad (wrong) or good (right) emotions, as they are all needed and part of our human experience, but rather to create awareness around emotional and vibrational consistency, so that no matter what happens in life, you aren't experiencing extreme highs and lows on the scale. Even if you do move down the scale you're able to move back up it authentically in a gentle and consistent way that honours all of your emotions and feels aligned and real to you.

Joy/Appreciation/Empowered/Freedom/Love
Passion
Enthusiasm / Eagerness / Happiness
Positive Expectation / Belief / Optimism
Hopefulness
Contentment
Boredom
Pessimism
Frustration/Irritation/Impatience
Overwhelmed
Dissapointment
Doubt
Worry
Blame
Discouragement
Anger/Revenge
Hatred/Rage
Jealousy
Isecurity/Guilt/Unworthiness
Fear/Grief/Despair/Powerlessness

The emotional scale

Energy

Alongside consistency, the second step is through working with your energy, and this part gets to be fun! As you'll see, the embodiment process that happens in this step is less about just "doing" and more about aligning. They say that energy is simply feelings in motion and I absolutely agree with this. To get us started, here are some simple suggestions for ways to raise your vibe. As with every tool or suggestion within this book, find what works for you. The best way to find what raises your vibration is by trying these out and seeing which ones feel expansive to your energy.

Nature: Getting outdoors and into the sunshine is a sure way to lift your vibration and mood as you soak up vitamin D. Even if it's not sunny, being able to connect to nature regulates your nervous system and allows you to be truly present. Get your bare feet on the grass if you can and spend even just 30 minutes in the sunshine and see how you feel afterwards.

Movement: Stuck and stagnant energy in your body not only lowers your vibration but stops you from feeling in alignment. Get moving your body through dance, walking, running or yoga, for example. All of these are fantastic for shifting emotions and energy through you to elevate your vibration.

Meditation: Whether it's a guided mediation on YouTube (I have one on my channel for raising your vibration) or your own freestyle version, meditation is a beautiful practice. It'll ground you, connect you back to your centre and help raise your vibration as you let go of any stress and anything no longer serving you. No matter what type you choose to do, meditation is a wonderful way to raise your vibration.

Crystals: Working with certain crystals can also help to raise your vibration. In particular, you can work with selenite, also known as the divine stone due to its strong resonance with the vibration of love, light and truth, to amplify other crystals' powers, or use it on its own to raise your frequency. Rose quartz is the stone of unconditional love and self-love, whose energy can instantly lift your mood and raise your vibration. Citrine is known as the manifestation stone and can help create balance and harmony in your life. Celestite is the angel stone and can help you connect to the angel realm and your spirit guides. Smokey quartz is a fantastic protective stone for clearing low vibrational energy from yourself and your energy field. Finally, amethyst is the perfect stone for raising your vibration during meditation and balancing your third eye chakra (for example, your intuition).

EFT: The emotional freedom technique, also called tapping, is a brilliant pain-free form of acupuncture using the meridian points of energy throughout the body. By tapping on certain meridian points with your fingers, you can release any stuck and stagnant energy from your body that is causing you to feel out of alignment or experience lower vibrations and emotions. You can see really quick shifts with this in only five or 10 minutes; I'd highly recommend searching for the king of EFT Brad Yates's videos on YouTube and giving this a try.

Gratitude: The quickest way to raise your vibration and feel positive regularly is through practising gratitude. Start by writing down three to five things you're grateful for in your journal and then your "why"; for example, "I'm so grateful for my home, because it's a beautiful space I love to spend my time in." See how you feel after doing this quick and easy practice. If it lifts your energy, why not include it in your morning routine to set yourself up for a positive day? Gratitude is the best attitude and what we're grateful for only multiplies in our lives. Gratitude is a great way to ground back in and tap into joy, appreciation and positivity.

Letting go of negativity: Whether it's decluttering your physical space, your emotions, people or the past, letting go of negativity and any spiritual clutter elevates the space around you and your vibration. Surrounding yourself with people, places and projects that inspire and uplift you will keep your vibration high and pick you up when you're feeling low. And vice versa: if your usually positive friend, for example, is going through a hard time, it's not about decluttering them because they're being negative; it's about honouring their emotions and being a comforting light for them during their challenges. We will be going into how to declutter physically, emotionally and spiritually in chapter 5.

Acts of kindness: We all hopefully know how it feels to do a small or random act of kindness for another person. Serving others with kindness and compassion raises both our vibration and theirs too. These small acts of generosity send a ripple effect of positivity and good vibes into the world. Selflessly giving to others from a place of abundance is incredibly powerful for raising your vibration and aligning with even more abundance, as the positive energy is reflected back to you.

Music and sound healing: Is there a particular song that makes you instantly feel uplifted and joyful when you hear it? Music has the incredible power to raise our vibration and help us feel good. Whether it's your favourite song or a healing sound bath, music has the ability to raise both your energy and your mood.

Nourishing your body: The food and drink we put in our body has the power to raise or lower our vibration. Now, I'm not going to suggest to you which foods are high vibrational or not, because you know your body better than me and, in all honesty, eating authentic pizza, risotto and arancini in Italy really did raise my vibration despite it being a carb fest! I believe in balance when it comes to food and in eating intuitively, as our bodies will let us know what they want! Also, look at how you feel after consuming alcohol; for me personally, it lowered my vibration massively, so I cut it out seven years ago now and I haven't looked back. Drinking plenty of water and making sure your body feels hydrated and loved is also a vibe raiser. Taking a salt bath is another great way to raise your vibration and clear any stagnant energy. I recommend using Epsom salts and pink Himalayan salt.

Sleep hygiene and habits: Finally, sleep hygiene and your daily habits play a huge role in your vibration and energy. Are you getting enough sleep? Or are you doom-scrolling on social media before bed and going to sleep in a stressed state? Scrolling before bed overstimulates the brain instead of relaxing and prepping it for rest. It'll be too busy processing all the information you're digesting; in fact, too much scrolling can actually trigger our fight or flight response in the nervous system. Try reading or even some meditation before bed to help you switch off and prepare for a great night's sleep. Look at your daily habits and even your morning routine to make sure these allow you to enter the day gently and support your happiness.

+ * +

As you'll discover in the next few chapters, when you feel emotionally regulated and consistently good within yourself, this second step will feel effortless. But for now, it's time to put these tips into action and create a vibrational practice that elevates your frequency and kick-starts the alignment process for you.

Aligned Actions

Action

Take a look at the list of tools and suggestions for raising your vibration on pages 25–7. Make a commitment over the coming weeks to do at least one or two of these vibe-raising practices a week. You can then build vibrational consistency through making these a devotional habit, which is also a great form of self-care! I like to map out in my diary which practices I can do that week to schedule time for them and set myself up for vibe-raising success.

Intention

For your intentional practice, I want you to focus on energy techniques to elevate your vibration. I have included my powerful "Raise Your Vibration" subliminal in the resources for this book on my website (see: www.emmamumford.co.uk/alignedabundance) to help you with raising your frequency and turning up your magnetism. Subliminals are positive affirmations created and read by myself, and put to healing-frequency music, so not only do you experience shifts from the affirmations, but healing from the sound frequencies in the music too. Although you may not hear the affirmations under the music, your subconscious mind can still absorb and process them, making this a magnetic way to reprogram any negative beliefs and manifest abundance. When repeating affirmations out loud, you may find that your conscious mind pipes up with blocks or resistance, which makes subliminals perfect for those who struggle to repeat positive affirmations about themselves or their desires because these feel unbelievable or farfetched. For me, this is one of my favourite ways to manifest, as you can pop these on in the background as little or as often as you like when working, cleaning, reading or even when brushing your teeth. However, they're not suitable to listen to when driving or operating heavy machinery, so please only listen to subliminals in a safe environment.

Journaling Prompts

- What raises my vibration and makes me feel good?
- What in my life is currently lowering my vibration?
- What consistency do I need to create in my life?
- What makes me feel my most magnetic self?
- How can I turn up my magnetism this week?

ALIGNED REFLECTIONS

- Nothing can switch off your magnetism or ability to manifest.
- The key to creating consistency with your manifestation and alignment practice is through intention, devotion and raising your vibration.
- When we have fun we raise our vibration and this in turn creates emotional and vibrational consistency, which reflects into our outer world as consistent habits, abundance or flow.
- Everything in this Universe, including humans, is thought to vibrate at different frequencies. These frequencies are influenced by our thoughts, emotions and actions.
- We don't live in a world of instantaneous manifestation, so not every thought or emotion will manifest into your life.
- Honouring your energy and emotions is important if you want to build a steady and solid base level of vibration.
- Raising your vibration means clearing any blocks or resistance to experiencing higher vibrations
- Surrounding yourself with people, places and projects that inspire and uplift you will keep your vibration high and pick you up when you're feeling low.

Create a Shift and Miracle

The metaphysical text *A Course in Miracles* defines a miracle not as some divine and gracious wonder bestowed upon us from the heavens above, but actually a shift in perception over a perceived problem. So rather than a miracle being something like the money materializing that you've been trying desperately to manifest to pay that unexpected bill, it's your shift from fear to love that creates the miracle so that creative solutions can manifest into your reality.

Often, when we're out of alignment and feeling stuck and stagnant in life, we need to kick-start the alignment process by creating a shift and change. This shift creates a ripple effect in our life, which then leads to a change in habits, routine and even in our energy, which results in a new outcome. As the famous saying goes, "Old ways won't open new doors." If you want to come into alignment with abundance in your life, you must be the catalyst for change. It always starts with us; we must move first and then the Universe matches us.

Let's use our radio station analogy again here: how can you expect to hear a different radio station playing your favourite song if you don't switch channel? You must change the frequency on the radio to align with your desired radio station where the songs align and you instantly feel like, "YASS, I have to listen – they're playing my favourite tune!" Alignment is your soul's song, and there's nothing sweeter than having found nothing exciting to listen to on the radio but then switching channels and coming across a song you haven't heard for years that instantly raises your vibration as you sing every single word! Remember, you have the power to change your frequency at any given moment, and creating a shift in your life is a sure way to jumpstart the alignment process and see aligned abundance and miracles flow into your life again.

I first read *A Course in Miracles* back in 2018 and it's definitely taken me some time to work through it all as it's not light reading! However, I do come back to its teachings time and time again when I need to shift from fear to love – and what I mean by love is joy, faith, trust and abundance. So often, we put the result of our miracles in the hands of the Universe, but while this is a co-creation process we must first ask for the miracle we're seeking and then follow the manifestation process to receive that miracle in our life.

Much to the confusion of some, the miracle itself is not the end result; and this is where I see so many people block their miracles by thinking that miracles lie outside of them, that they're God-given or granted by the Universe – that it's out of their hands. Spiritual solutions are actually ever-present and it's only when we get caught up in the perceived problem that we're blinded from seeing these. A miracle means shifting into the knowing that everything starts from within, that spiritual solutions have always shown up for us (and always will) and that the Universe's love is always present.

The Universe Always has our Back

I want you to think back to a time in your life when you REALLY needed a miracle or solution, a time when you had absolutely no idea when or how a miracle would happen. But then it did. Reflect for a moment on that process. What was that miracle? How did it show up? How did the Universe support you?

When we reflect on past experiences of miracles and creative solutions, we can see evidence that we are magnets for miracles and that there's always a solution to a perceived problem. I use the word "perceived" as often when we're in the thick of it in the day-to-day issues that can arise like unexpected bills, your landlord suddenly selling your home, your car breaking down right before a really important trip – you know what I'm talking about, right? – it's times like those that can instantly send your nervous system spiralling into anxiety, fear and a feeling of "what the hell do I do?!" Well, this is the perfect time to call upon a miracle.

From our perspective, we see the problem right in front of us causing these road blocks, fear and panic. Yet, from the Universe's perspective, it can see the *whole* picture and must think, "Gosh, I just saved you from being involved in a car accident and you're panicking?" Or, "But I really wanted you to have the dream house you've been putting on your vision board and now it's come up, I need you to be on the lookout for a property – yet you're fearful!"

Okay, obviously the Universe doesn't think like this. The Universe sees the solution and *why* something needed to happen, as disruptive as that may feel to us. When we ask for a miracle, we are opening up to opportunities to up-level, shift and align with a higher and more vibrant timeline. So although your car breaking down may wind you up all day, it could have just saved your from being somewhere at the wrong time – there are no mistakes. Today, when I'm running late, there's traffic or something gets cancelled, I thank the Universe and know it's protected me from something.

An example of this happened for me back in 2023, when I was excited to manifest a trip to Rome and Greece. Yet, no matter what my partner and I did, as soon as I went to book it something would happen. We couldn't find dog care and then there were terrible wild fires around Greece. Yes, you guessed it: the brand-new hotel we were planning to book was one of the only hotels in Rhodes to be severely damaged and it closed immediately. Thank you, Universe, for keeping us safe. Okay, I thought, I'll book our trip for later in the season. So I went to book the holiday in September, but it still didn't feel right. Then poor Greece experienced severe floods. To prove the Universe always has our backs, the same week we would have booked our holiday, the car park at the London airport was set on fire, damaging hundreds of cars where ours would have been parked. I kid you not, my ever-sceptical partner couldn't believe this series of events all unfolding one after the other during the times we were meant to be travelling.

At the time, I felt sad I couldn't enjoy travelling that year, but we'd just moved into our beautiful first home, so I used the time to focus on the garden and enjoy living in our house. If we'd been travelling, I genuinely don't think I would have enjoyed the first few months here as much as I did.

During this time, I took a two-month sabbatical from my business to rest and refill my cup. That was when some suppressed childhood trauma came up for me that I'd had no previous awareness of, and it rocked my world entirely. Thank God I was home when this happened and not on holiday, sitting there feeling triggered and crying on a foreign beach. I was SO thankful I was home, safe, off work and had the time and space to unpack this with my therapist. Looking back, I know wholeheartedly the Universe had my back that summer and I was exactly where I needed to be.

Now, I accept that my example of a cancelled holiday isn't the biggest problem in the world, because I could just book one again when everything aligned, but you can see how it could have been easy to panic and get upset over the perceived problem; but because I surrendered to the constant doors closing, spiritual solutions arrived.

When we're talking about more serious and life-threatening problems, or a loved one desperately needing a miracle, this is very different and of course a very valid concern. Miracles in these cases can still be a spiritual solution, but situations like these offer an invitation to surrender and to let the Universe usher in whatever is for the highest good for that person.

Is there a Limit to How Many Miracles We Can Receive?

Just like abundance, miracles know no bounds or limits, and there's no limit to the number of miracles you can receive. But before we ask the Universe for a miracle, we must first check in to see *why* we need this miracle. If there isn't an obvious emergency, we have to look internally as to whether the miracle we want is actually filling a void. For example, are you seeking a miracle in your love life, like a dream partner manifesting for you, yet you don't feel self-love? Instead, you might feel shame, self-loathing or doubt your self-worth. In this instance, the miracle isn't about your dream partner manifesting; it's the aligned action you need take to align with the reality you want to attract.

Think about it: the version of you who has this relationship in their life, would they feel shame, self-loathing or doubt their self-worth? Would you really want to feel those emotions when you're madly in love and happy? No! So the miracle is really your shift in perception around the problem. Your aligned action is asking for the miracle and then working on yourself, healing these aspects that aren't in alignment with your desired reality and embodying the version of yourself who *is* happy and aligned with that relationship. Then, as is if by magic, the miracle will appear in the form of your dream partner. Remember that it's not about the end result; it's all about the process and how you shift so that you can facilitate this miracle in your life.

"Okay," I hear you say. "If that's the case and miracles are limitless, then why aren't they pouring into our lives on a daily basis?" Well, the truth is that they are present every single day in weird and wonderful ways. Miracles and shifts often occur on a mundane level, yet we might not even notice them, because we very often hold little or no attachment to them. For example, imagine that work calls up and they need you to come in urgently, as your dream client has moved the meeting to today. You're panicking about childcare and having the time to pull everything together, but then your mum calls up out of the blue, offering to take the kids, and it all aligns perfectly. There's an everyday miracle, right there!

Ask for Support from Your Spirit Team

Your spirit team are a collection of spiritual guides, such as spirit guides, guardian angels, ancestors, animal totems or deities, believed to provide guidance, support and protection throughout your life. These energies are unique to each person and can be connected with through practices like meditation, intention or journaling.

We often hold more attachment to the bigger and more important sorts of miracles, which means they can become blocked or stagnant more easily if we're not taking aligned and inspired action toward them. The Universe and our spirit team can't step in and interfere on our behalf, as we live in a world of free will, which means that we must open up to miracles and actively ask for their support. Once we set that intention, our spirit team and the Universe can get to work by putting the right people and opportunities in front of us that can help manifest the miracle or desire we want.

So why can't the Universe just step in if it can see we're struggling, and we're in need of a miracle or stuck? The answer is we all have soul contracts and karmic lessons we've chosen to learn here in this lifetime, which can even be seen through our personal astrology and numerology. If the Universe was like an overbearing parent who stepped in and solved every problem for you before you even had a chance to think, would you learn anything? Would you up-level and receive the lesson you've come here to learn and embody? Probably not! This is why your spirit team can only step in once you give them permission. As it's their main priority to support and guide you here in this lifetime, call upon them in moments of need and if you need a helping hand to show you the next best step. You don't need to see the whole staircase at this point – that's not how alignment works – you just need to know your next best step.

Manifesting Miracles for Others

Another question I often get asked is whether we can manifest miracles for other people – and, yes, we absolutely can! I like to think of manifesting miracles for others as a sort of prayer to the Universe, where we must detach from the outcome and pray for a creative solution for the highest good. As with any manifestation, we must always say, "This or something better for the highest good of all", when manifesting for others. As lovely as it is to want to manifest a miracle for another, we can't always see the bigger picture and we can't interfere with others' free will and destiny. At the end of the day, you don't want to manifest something for someone that could make their situation even worse. All you can do is set the intention for the highest good and allow the Universe to take care of the finer details.

Manifesting miracles for others is a great introduction into how we can expand our awareness around miracles themselves and take our manifestation game even deeper. I recommend doing this with all of your manifestations, but let's concentrate on miracles for now. Think about how your miracle can positively impact the collective. When we go from the mindset of "What can I get out of this?" into 'How will the world benefit from my miracle?", we shift into an expanded mindset where we're thinking of others and the ripple effect that manifesting has on the wider world. The truth is all our manifestations have a knock-on effect in the world, but how often do we take the time to think about this and why we're manifesting our desires? When we turn the focus away from simply what we'll benefit from, we open up to unconditional love and oneness in the knowledge that our abundance can positively impact others, too. Think about how your miracle can positively impact those around you and the whole collective ...

Blocks to Miracles

Let's dive into more of the shadow side of miracles and why we block miracles from flowing into our life. Belief certainly plays a big factor in blocking miracles, and this can be broken down into belief in ourselves and in the Universe to manifest this solution in our life. Without belief, the Universe can't get to work as, remember, the divine mirror of life is always reflecting back to us our beliefs and energy. If you're showing up in front of the mirror of life with doubt and fearful energy, guess what's going to be reflected back to you? (We'll go deeper into my belief process for aligned abundance in chapter 8.)

Another way miracles can become blocked is through attachment. When we're desperate for a shift or miracle to occur in our lives, it's only natural we should care about this and want it to happen. But staying attached to the outcome and to that miracle only keeps it further away. There's a quote from *A Course in Miracles* that I always remind myself of when feeling attached to an outcome: "Infinite patience produces immediate results." To break this down, it essentially means that needing nothing attracts everything. Just like with your manifestations, miracles will happen when you need them the least. This can sound very contradictory when you read my five steps to manifesting and have gone along the process of getting clear, clearing any resistance, taking aligned action – and now I'm suggesting that you let it all go and don't even think about needing the desired outcome anymore?! It's a difficult one to get your head around, which is why "let go", my fourth step in the five-step process, is one of the hardest for people to embody, as they can feel so deeply attached to their desires.

But to stay with the topic of miracles, when we can show up with infinite patience for miracles, solutions can manifest instantly. Remember the divine mirror: how would the version of yourself who has this miracle in their life be showing up in front of that mirror? Would they be calm, relaxed and trusting, or fearful, anxious and feeling lack? Work on embodying the very feelings you'd experience when you have your desire, as this is the quickest way to align with the frequency of your miracle and welcome it into your life. (I will go into more about embodying your desires together in chapter 13, "Embody the Abundant Version of Yourself".)

Another common block I see with miracles is the fear of receiving them. Let's face it, receiving the very thing you've asked for can be scary, especially if it's the shift you've been asking for in your life, or the money for that project you've been desperate to start for years, for example. It challenges you to up-level, meaning there are no more excuses – it's go time!

Reassuring your body and nervous system daily that it's safe to receive miracles is a great way to make sure you're not feeding the fear or self-doubt. Another aspect to this is whether your body feels safe enough to receive the miracle, as our nervous system can do a great job of pushing away abundance and the very things we want if it feels this will stress us or cause harm. (I'll share more on the science of this in the next chapter.)

Which leads us on to space, as we know that with manifesting you must have the space in your life to manifest new abundance and energy – and the same goes for miracles. Do you have the space in your life to hold and sustain this miracle or shift? We'll be diving into this more deeply together in chapter 5, "Declutter Your Energy and Life", but it's worth realizing now that creating the space in your life for miracles and shifts to occur is vital in the alignment process.

Manifest a Miracle

Now you know the basics of miracles and how these can show up in your life, it's time to manifest a shift and miracle right now! Setting a powerful intention like this near the start of your aligned abundance journey is going to have huge results for you, as we go deeper into the process. So, if you've been feeling stuck in a manifesting rut or bogged down in a season of your life for a while, get ready for the Universe to show you how good it gets to be when you stay open to creative solutions and take aligned action toward your miracle.

Remember that when setting an intention for a miracle with the Universe, you want to be specific, clear and know your "why". For example, if your miracle is to shift from feeling low, your why could be to experience happiness and joy again, as this will positively impact those around you too. Or if your miracle is to manifest £500 to pay an unexpected car bill, your why could be to be able to carry on using your car and have access to easy transport. This will have a knock-on effect collectively, as the local garage you use to repair the car will be able to meet their bills and pay their staff, and you'll be able to drive yourself around safely. Finally, if you're manifesting a shift in your current circumstances, your why could be to shift into a better position at work, which would light you up more and, collectively, you'd be able to help more people from this aligned role. In turn, this could bring your company more business, as you'd feel even more passionate about this new role. The possibilities of your why personally and collectively are endless; journal down what you think yours could be as you start to get clear on what your miracle intention is.

You may have had a miracle or shift come straight to mind as you've been reading this chapter, or you still may not have a clue what miracle you want to manifest! I've got you covered: below, you'll find my life wheel, a version of which features in all of my books, and which we'll call the aligned abundance wheel here.

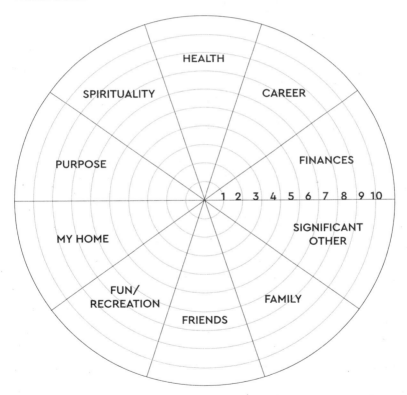

The aligned abundance wheel

Make a copy of this aligned abundance wheel (or print one off from the resources at www.emmamumford.co.uk/alignedabundance), then colour it in or write down your score for each area of your life, rating this from 1 to 10, with 1 being "I don't feel aligned or abundant in that area" and 10 being "I feel fully aligned and abundant". I'm getting you to do this before you set your miracle intention, so you can establish which areas may feel the most stuck or stagnant in your life and in turn, get some clarity on what your miracle could be. Take some time to colour in this life wheel and reflect on each score afterwards. Did anything surprise you with your scores? Then reflect upon what would make any low scores a 10: what would the miracle or shift be? (If you're aiming for more of a general shift in your life rather than a specific miracle, this can look like movement, opportunities, progress, flow, ease or creative solutions; just tap into whichever word most aligns with the shift you're seeking.)

Once you have an idea of your miracle intention or shift, it's time to declare this to the Universe. There are many incredible ways to set an intention with the Universe, whether it's through saying it out loud, writing it down, creating a vision board or meditating on it, for example; but for this miracle experiment, you can simply write down the miracle intention below, tweak it to suit your intention and then repeat it out loud. Yes, it really is as simple as that!

Universe, I call upon you to help bring this miracle [insert your miracle] into my life now for the highest good of all. I trust you to align me with the right people, places and opportunities to help manifest creative solutions and miracles in my life. I welcome in these miracles and solutions with ease. Thank you, thank you, thank you, Universe.

Once you've repeated the above, take a deep breath in and let it all go on the exhale. That's it – you've done the hardest part, which is getting clear and setting the intention!

Open Up to Receiving Miracles

Now, a few minutes may have passed since setting your intention and you may already be thinking, "Great, so where's my miracle, Emma?" Your next step involves shifting into receiving your miracle and taking aligned action. You only need ask once for your miracle, so we won't be focusing on repeating any affirmations or practices as such; instead, I really want you to get into the energy of receiving and opening up to divine miracles.

The first way you can start to open up to miracles is by creating a change. As the famous saying goes, "Nothing changes if nothing changes." If we want to help co-create a miracle in our life, we must do something different – which could simply mean seeing a situation from a new perspective or responding to a challenge in a new way. A great example of this is if your miracle involves another person. If the same argument or frustration keeps arising for you, it's time to try a new approach or do something different. A great affirmation I love to use in this type of manifesting miracles is:

"I choose to see this differently. Universe help me to see this situation through the lens of love."

The same old intention plus action won't equal a new outcome. It may sound simple, but by stopping the cycle from repeating, we open up the space for shifts, miracles and creative solutions to occur. When we make more aligned decisions and actions, this up-levels our energy, which in turn shows the Universe that, "Yes, I am choosing differently this time", which means the Universe can get to work and usher in the solutions.

Stopping the cycles and patterns that aren't serving us is vital in the alignment process, as if we want to see change we must *be* the change. It all starts from within – so that one small decision or change in your actions could have a huge ripple effect in your life, which magnetizes endless miracles to you. If you want better, you must decide you deserve better. Your beliefs match your actions, so if you're scared to choose differently or worried what the response might be from the other person, know that by choosing better they will step up and match this new energy if it's for their own highest good.

Once you make this sort of change, no matter how big or small, your life will begin to change, too, as the Universe gets to work and brings abundance to you to match this new reality. Even if the change is about shifting from fear to love in the process of manifesting a money miracle, for example, these small shifts all add up to the miracle, which as we know, is a shift in how we see the situation.

Remember that you can't force miracles; we're flowing, not forcing! Maintaining an attitude of neutrality toward the Universe and your miracle is important, as you want to stay surrendered and in the energy of receiving. This is achievable through building trust in the Universe and staying flexible in the unfolding of this manifestation. The more flowing you are with your miracles and creative solutions, the more effortless they will feel. (I'll be going through my ultimate guide to building unwavering trust in yourself and the Universe in chapter 8.) Asking for a miracle requires us to surrender to the divine and trust that both the Universe and our spirit team will support us and provide us with the next steps along our path. If you're asking for a shift in your life during this chapter, it means believing that this shift and change are possible, and being open to receiving them.

One great tip I love to share at my live talks to get the audience into the energy of receiving is to ask, "How often do you allow yourself to receive?" This could be love, money, gifts or support, for example, because very often we can be incredibly giving to our loved ones yet forget that we too need to receive. I used to have an uncomfortable relationship with receiving gifts; on birthdays and at Christmas, I'd always feel awkward unwrapping gifts though I loved buying gifts for my family. After looking into my own relationship with receiving and uncovering the belief beneath this, now I allow myself to receive support, gifts and so much more than I used to, and I know it's safe to allow myself to receive. Now my abundance and manifestations flow almost effortlessly each and every time, as I'm in the energy of receiving regularly. So I want you to challenge yourself to receive more this week. Whether it involves asking for help, letting your friend pay for coffee if they offer, allowing your partner to make dinner so you can put your feet up, give yourself permission to receive goodness, Queen! When we open up to the energy of receiving, we open up to receiving incredible abundance and miracles in our life.

In any moment, your life can completely change and that is the beauty of miracles: an "aha!" moment or a shift in your perception can create a whole new reality and movement forward. So now that you've set your miracle intention, stay open, get comfortable with receiving, remain surrendered and know that somehow and in some way the miracle will always come. Your miracle or creative solution may appear instantly as you move through the chapters in this book, or it may be the very last cherry on top of the cake as you finish reading. Everyone's miracle will be different, so trust in the timing and that you are worthy and deserving of miracles – because you truly are! Let go of timeframes and relax into the tasks and aligned actions suggested at the end of this chapter to help magnetize miracles into your life.

Aligned Actions

Action

Using the aligned abundance wheel in this chapter, look at each area of your life and colour this in or write your scores in your journal. Rate each area on a scale of 1 to 10 (with 1 meaning you don't feel very abundant or aligned in that area and 10 meaning you feel incredibly aligned and abundant). Once you've finished, spend some time reflecting on whether any areas have surprised you. Next, it's time to reflect on what will make these areas feel like a 10. Looking at your scores, what would make them a 10? Write down some actionable goals or intentions to help manifest more alignment in these areas, moving forward.

Intention

Set your miracle intention with the mantra given earlier in this chapter and make sure to write it down in your journal so you don't forget what you've asked for. This will also help you keep track of the aligned abundance that manifests with each chapter of the book.

Journaling Prompts

- How can I allow myself to receive more this week?
- What is my relationship like with receiving? (*Describe it.*)
- What is my miracle intention or shift I'd like to see in my life?
- How does it feel to receive miracles?
- What miracles or creative solutions have I received in the past? (*List as many as you can.*)

ALIGNED REFLECTIONS

- Remember that you have the power to change your frequency at any given moment. Creating a shift and miracle in your life is a sure way to jumpstart the alignment process and see aligned abundance flow into your life again.
- Miracles have no bounds or limits, and there's no limit to the number of miracles you can receive. Just like abundance, they're limitless.
- It's not about the end result, it's all about the process and how you shift so that you can facilitate this miracle in your life.
- Manifesting miracles for others is a great introduction into how we can expand our awareness around miracles and take our manifestation game even deeper.
- When we can show up with an infinite patience for miracles, solutions can manifest instantly.
- Stopping the cycles and patterns that aren't serving us is vital in the alignment process, as if we want to see change we must be the change.
- Asking for a miracle requires us to surrender to the divine and trust that both the Universe and our spirit team will support us and guide us on the next steps along our path.
- When we open up to the energy of receiving, we open up to receiving incredible abundance and miracles in our life.

Manifest from a Place
of Regulation

I'm often asked what my favourite manifestation has been over my nine-year manifestation journey and I always answer, "My peace and healing." Yes, the dream house, dream relationship, our Dachshund Luna, money, holidays and things like that are all incredible, and I'm deeply grateful and humbled to have manifested so many wonderful things over the years. But if you asked me on a deeper level, I'd tell you this: when I spiritually awakened back in 2016, I'd been experiencing depression and anxiety for nearly a decade. I was miserable, I had no idea how to love myself and I was so, so sad. To be here nearly a decade on from that point and to be feeling happy, fulfilled and at peace is the biggest miracle I could have ever asked for. The peace I feel within my heart and soul are the greatest wealth I could have in this lifetime.

The reason I'm sharing this with you is because I've noticed how my level of abundance and ease with manifestation has changed over the years. In the beginning, it felt like an uphill struggle to manifest my biggest desires and I'd often hit hurdles, blocks and setbacks. The journey honestly felt exhausting sometimes. Even when I'd manifest those desires I wanted, I'd still feel anxious and it wouldn't bring me peace. I learned through my last relationship, which I'd also manifested, that the Universe would never bring me peace in something I wasn't meant to settle in. I wasn't manifesting aligned abundance;

I was manifesting desires that matched my level of trauma at that moment in time.

You see, as I went along my healing journey (which I document in my book *Hurt, Healing, Healed*), I realized two things: (1), that I'd spent most of my life operating from an unregulated nervous system and didn't know what regulation meant; and (2), that I no longer wanted to manifest the same things that I'd wanted at the beginning of my journey. As I was healing and up-levelling so were my dreams and manifestations. I was now manifesting more aligned abundance, which reflected my new energy and vibration, and felt truly in alignment with my soul.

What I also came to notice through therapy and other healing modalities, was the more I learned to relax and regulate my nervous system, the better choices I was making, my anxiety and depression healed and my body finally started healing, too. I could finally breathe easy and feel safe in my body. I was able to process my emotions in a more grounded way and most importantly, manifest from a regulated space.

Manifestation is a mind, body, spirit experience, so to bring our desires into reality we have to bring them into the body; and if you're feeling unregulated, anxious or overwhelmed, what effect do you think this will have on your desires? Your manifestations should relax and bring your nervous system and body peace. Regulation absolutely deserves its own chapter, as the peace I feel now is available to every single person; and being able to operate from a regulated and grounded space when manifesting is vital to ensure you set aligned intentions and receive aligned abundance.

What is the Nervous System?

In biology, the nervous system includes the brain, spinal cord and a complex network of nerves. This system sends messages back and forth between the brain and different parts of the body. It contains threadlike nerves that branch out to every organ and body part. The human body's nervous system can be divided into two main parts: the central nervous system (CNS) and the peripheral nervous system, both of which can be further subdivided.

The voluntary (or somatic) nervous system: This is the part of the peripheral nervous system that handles our bodily movements. The peripheral nervous system connects the brain to motor neurons, which control our sensory neurons, muscles and glands. It's responsible for converting external stimuli from our environment into internal electrical impulses, and connect to the muscles that are under our conscious control.

The involuntary (or autonomic) nervous system: This part of the peripheral nervous system works without you even thinking about it and regulates the function of your internal organs, such as your stomach, lungs and heart. Essentially, it keeps your body going without you having to do anything about it, even while you sleep! Within the involuntary nervous system, there are two main branches:

- the sympathetic nervous system – arousing (fight or flight)
- the parasympathetic nervous system – calming (rest/ digest/heal)

The nervous system's primary role is to protect and keep us alive; it only cares about external threats and how they impact our safety. The subconscious mind works alongside the nervous system to do just this and doesn't care about our personal growth or evolution. The conscious mind (the discerning mind) will go quiet when a threat is detected, meaning we can't think logically, intuitively or creatively if our nervous system is out of alignment. This impacts our decision-making, emotions and the reality we perceive. This is why it's always important to check in with your aligned decisions and make sure you are making decisions from a place of love, not fear.

In manifestation, the nervous system determines whether our manifestations are lasting or fleeting. Many mystics have also said it's the bridge that connects the soul. When the subconscious mind perceives a threat, it then sends signals to the nervous system to go into survival mode. This is why when manifesting, I recommend asking yourself, "Does this [person/job/house/friendship/investment] calm my nervous system?" Remember that emotions are energy in motion, so if your nervous system perceives your desires to be a threat or dangerous, then guess what? Your subconscious mind and body will start to sabotage you physically and energetically to keep the perceived threat as far away from you as possible. This can materialize as limiting beliefs, fears, blocks, resistance and trauma. If you've been struggling to take aligned action or make aligned decisions toward your desires, chances are your nervous system doesn't currently feel safe holding that desire. (If you'd like to learn more about the nervous system, I have included a couple of great books in the resources section on page 225.)

HOW TO IDENTIFY AN UNBALANCED NERVOUS SYSTEM

Now we know what the nervous system is and how it impacts our ability to hold and sustain our desires, the good news is we can balance and keep the nervous system calm, happy and aligned – even when uncertainty or challenges arise in life. So what does an unregulated and regulated nervous system look like? Below, I've included some common signs that can help you to identify whether your nervous system is operating in a place of harmony and balance, or whether it's operating from a stress response:

Unregulated nervous system: feeling tired, sluggish, unmotivated, over reactive, snappy, experiencing emotional rollercoasters, trouble sleeping, struggling to make decisions, tense, lethargic and foggy memory.

Regulated nervous system: finding emotions easy to regulate, calm, flowing, present, motivated, optimistic, engaged, adaptive, social, inspired and creative.

Balancing Your Nervous System

Once you can balance your nervous system, you'll find that your body will be so much happier, your mindset will thrive and that the things that used to trigger you or make you feel anxious will no longer have the same impact. The goal with balancing your nervous system is not to be perfect and experience zero stress for ever more, but rather to be able to handle and respond to situations in an aligned way that feels right for you. As someone who lived with anxiety and depression for over a decade of their life, balancing my nervous system has been life-changing for me in terms of my hormones, happiness and the level of aligned abundance in my life. Now, I'm able to tackle problems from a much more grounded place, rather than feeling anxious and unable to function or cope.

Balancing your nervous system is a consistent commitment – to ease, to faith in the Universe and to your peace. You can start to balance your nervous system by using various somatic practices and tools. While these physical actions will be deeply transformational, it's also important to address any root emotions, triggers and trauma, as this will have the most long-lasting impact on your nervous system. I would recommend working with a therapist, or an EMDR (eye movement desensitization and reprocessing) psychotherapist. EMDR has been life-changing for my nervous system and it's a fantastic way to regulate and process any past emotions or traumas. My third book, *Hurt, Healing, Healed*, can also help you to identify root emotions or blocks and to begin to process these.

Coming into balance in your mind, body and spirit is the ultimate form of alignment. When you can bring balance into the nervous system, you can start to make aligned decisions and choices from your intuition rather than based on emotion. Below are some somatic practices to help you start to regulate the nervous system as well as raising your vibration. I've already touched upon a couple of these, such as the healing power of nature, sleep and EFT, but they're so important for the nervous system that it's worth mentioning them again.

Nature and sunshine: Try to get at least half an hour of sunshine and fresh air a day. This will help you to manage your stress levels while you soak up vitamin D, which encourages serotonin production and is key to boosting mood and inner balance. Research also suggests that vitamin D is linked to reducing anxiety and is essential for a happy and healthy central nervous system.

Turn down the volume of life: This is essential for a regulated nervous system. Noise sensitivity is very common in unregulated nervous systems. Think about what type of music you're listening to and ask yourself, "Does this calm my nervous system?" The same goes for TV shows. Similarly, when you're out and about, choose places and content carefully to ensure your nervous system feels supported and at ease. Overwhelm can also stress our nervous system, so maybe turning down the volume means saying no to more and allowing your nervous system time to relax and breathe instead. It's important to avoid any unnecessary stimuli so that the parasympathetic nervous system (which is responsible for the body's rest and digestion response) can be active.

Hug and embrace: Whether it's your pet, a loved one or yourself, hugging and touch release endorphins and oxytocin, which promote happiness and pleasure. So bring it on for a hug!

Ground yourself: This is essential when raising your vibration and regulating the nervous system. Either lie under a weighted blanket or walk barefoot in nature to help relieve anxiety and ground you back into your body and into the present moment.

Make time to go with the flow: If you always have a busy schedule, where is your time for fun, joy and flow? Make sure you have space in your day and week to go slow if needs be and for self-care and activities that feed your soul.

Shake it off: Listening to Taylor Swift's song with the same title while shaking it all off is optional but highly recommended, as literally shaking your body about is a great way to regulate and release stuck or stagnant emotions!

Take cold plunges: I'm a huge fan of the Wim Hof Method and you can listen to Wim's inspirational story and advice on cold water therapy over on my Spiritual Queen's Badass Podcast. Now, I'm not one for cold showers, so you won't find me doing those regularly, but taking ice baths, cold plunges and showers two to three times a week can have huge benefits, including reduced inflammation in the body. Studies have even linked cold plunging to treating depression and improving mood. It can boost levels of dopamine and endorphins, creating alertness and happiness – which equals a happy nervous system. I love doing these at the spa and have even contemplated getting a cold-plunge inflatable pool for home. Honestly, give this a go and see how different you feel afterwards. Have a look into the Wim Hof Method to learn how to get started and also how to use breathwork to help with cold plunges.

Get a good night's sleep: Getting at least eight hours' sleep is the answer to most of our beauty and health ailments. Having a good sleep hygiene routine will not only ease any anxiety before bed but set up your nervous system for success the next day. Remove any stimulating distractions before bed to help you to get sleep more quickly and to sleep more deeply.

Do breathwork: One of my favourite tools for calming the nervous system is breathwork. Deep breathing and relaxation activate the parasympathetic nervous system, which sends a signal to your brain to tell you that you're safe and don't need to use the fight, flight or freeze response. Deep breathing also gets more oxygen to the brain, which helps your body to feel supported and secure. Breathwork is a great embodiment tool for bringing your manifestation into your body and to show the nervous system it's safe to hold this abundance.

EFT: Once again, EFT (emotional freedom technique) is a great tool for shifting energy. By tapping into certain meridian points on your body with your hand, you can release stuck and stagnant energy from your body that causes you to feel stressed or in a flight or fight mode. This is my absolute go-to when I feel unregulated or anxious.

Try yoga: This is one of my favourite somatic practices, which instantly relaxes and grounds me. Studies have shown that yoga can also help with prevention of cardiac diseases. The health benefit I find that pops up the most is yoga's ability to maintain good autonomic nervous system (ANS) balance. Another way that yoga soothes the nervous system is through pranayama or breathing techniques. Child's pose especially is great to do daily to release stress, ground into your body and maintain balance in the nervous system.

Child's pose in yoga

Go walking: A good walk can help to boost your mood because it increases blood flow and blood circulation to the brain and body. It has a positive influence on your hypothalamic-pituitary-adrenal (HPA) axis, which is your central nervous response system. This is beneficial because the HPA axis is responsible for your stress response, which means you'll be able to respond to any stressful situations from a more balanced and calm state.

Cut down on caffeine and sugar: This was a big culprit in my own unbalanced nervous system; I would feel my anxiety get worse and I'd often feel extremely drowsy after drinking caffeine. I personally chose to cut out caffeine over five years ago now and haven't looked back. I also try to keep my sugar consumption as low as possible to help my nervous system to feel calm. Caffeine stimulates the release of stress hormones, which can produce increased levels of anxiety, irritability, muscular tension and pain, indigestion, insomnia, and decreased immunity. It also acts on neurotransmitters in the brain that slow down the nervous system and cause drowsiness. If you've been struggling with anxiety, sleep or digestive problems for a length of time, then consider drinking coffee or highly caffeinated drinks later in the morning or an hour after breakfast, as this will help to balance your cortisol levels (cortisol being a hormone that activates the body's stress response).

Manifest from a Regulated Space

So now we've had a bit of a biology lesson in how the nervous system works on a practical level, it's time to bring this into manifestation and why we need to be manifesting from a regulated space. When our nervous system is calm and relaxed, we're able to make aligned decisions from our intuition, not emotion. This means that when setting intentions, you operate from a peaceful and balanced space that allows your soul's desires to come through and manifest.

When you're in the space of unregulated energy, you're setting intentions fuelled by emotions and are manifesting through your limiting beliefs, fears and trauma. This is why when you heal your nervous system and do the inner work, you'll very often find that you no longer want the same things that you once desired. This isn't a negative, though; it's actually a positive, as you shift into your soul's alignment and actually manifest the things you really do want, not desires that will cause you stress or anxiety.

When your nervous system is unbalanced or stressed, especially for prolonged periods of time, this lowers your vibration and blocks the manifestation process. The longer we avoid our emotions, the longer they will sit in our energy field and body, and can eventually manifest into our reality.

Now, that being said, we do need our emotions if we're to manifest our desires! We need positive emotions such as joy, love and happiness to help bring our desires into reality. So while lower vibrational emotions such as fear, unhappiness or sadness impact our vibration and our ability to manifest, when we can align with positive, higher frequency emotions to connect to our desires, we will become a vibrational match for them and those very same emotions will manifest into our reality. Manifesting is all about energy and, as we know, emotion is energy in motion, meaning that manifestation is an emotional experience and we can tap into our emotions to create our reality both consciously and unconsciously.

This is why I always advise you FEEL when manifesting; don't just set an intention of "I'd like to manifest £10,000", or "I'd like to manifest a dream relationship". The Universe is always responding to your energy; so sure, you might manifest both of those things with ease, but if they make you feel like crap or you find that you're actually unhappy in that dream relationship or with all that money, then what was it all for? You don't want to manifest an object or a person; you want to manifest a feeling or experience. Instead, focus on how you want to feel with that desire and let those feelings be your guide in this process.

When to Stop, Reset and Realign

Manifesting should be fun and, if it's not, remember my alignment protocol and stop, reset and realign (see page 17)! It should be something that lights your soul up, feels joyful, expansive, positive and brings aligned abundance to you. If it's feeling like a drag or you feel like you've fallen off the bandwagon, then I invite you to look at how this might be impacting your nervous system, too. Do your manifestations feel flowing? Or are they feeling forced? Most importantly, is what you're doing now relaxing your nervous system?

If you know that what you're doing currently – whether that's a daily practice, manifesting rituals or aligned action – is stressing you out, then stop, reset and realign. If it's stressing you out and causing anxiety, look at where you may need to support your nervous system, so you can realign in a way that creates sustainability, consistency and an environment where your body can thrive.

Does It Feel Safe To Have Your Desire?

I'll always remember Brad Yates, the king of EFT (emotional freedom technique) and legendary YouTuber, delivering an incredible workshop for my Manifestation Membership in 2020. In it, he explained that the reason why limiting beliefs and fears are blocking our desires is because at some level it doesn't feel safe for us to have this desire. This changed my whole outlook on blocks and fears; and once again, if your nervous system doesn't feel safe, it's going to do everything in its power to protect you, i.e., keep your manifestation well away from you!

I want you to sit with this idea and explore whether your desires feel safe to you and your body. If not, don't worry: through regulation and the inner work you can rewire your subconscious and nervous system to know that your desires are safe and calming to your body.

The subconscious mind controls your life 95 per cent of the time, with your conscious mind only being in control for 5 per cent of it (this being the part of your mind that is present here with me, reading this book). Which is wild when you think about how the part of your mind that you access day in, day out only makes up such a small percentage of your mind in total! In manifestation, this explains how the subconscious mind is running the show and creating 95 per cent of your reality.

Another fear that I see when it comes to feeling safe around your desire is the fear of screwing it up. Sometimes it's not just about your desire manifesting that scares your nervous system; it can actually be a fear around getting it wrong, making a mess of things and even losing your desire. So your nervous system could be protecting you from further loss, pain and disappointment.

What I've come to learn over the years of regulating my nervous system is that you can do all the somatic practices that I've recommended above, but if you're not addressing the root cause or limiting beliefs, the trauma will still be there. Work on the inner world and you'll see how your nervous system starts to relax and trusts that your abundance *is* safe.

Manifesting Something Out of Alignment

I want to dive a little deeper into how manifesting unaligned desires impacts our nervous system (and why I wrote *Aligned Abundance* in the first place). Manifesting unaligned desires in our life triggers the body and nervous system; this is why when that "dream relationship" manifests you feel anxious or stressed. This is your body's way of saying "it's not for you". It can be hard sometimes to know whether the date in front of you or the miracle job offer is your manifestation, but it comes back to "you'll know it's meant for you by the way it feels": your nervous system will tell you whether this is your desire or not.

An example of this was when I manifested my first "dream man" and I felt anxious and stressed. I had hormonal imbalances and my body was screaming to me that this was not really my dream man – but I ignored the red flags, I ignored the anxiety in my body and went along in that relationship for three years more than I should have done. Now, I accept I obviously had lessons to learn there, to do with soul contracts, and I finally dove into inner work after this break-up, so the relationship definitely needed to happen. However, when I met my now fiancé I felt completely different. Meeting him felt relaxing and easy; yet because there weren't butterflies in my stomach, instant passion or intensity, and my nervous system felt calm, to me at that time it meant "not my guy". Our relationship was a slow-burn and I'm so thankful it was, as it showed me what a healthy, happy relationship should look like; and the peace I felt was the biggest sign that this was my aligned abundance, not the anxiety and stress I'd felt before. I felt so safe around my fiancé when we met and I instantly relaxed; again, this was my body's way of showing me it was my desire.

The reason why I'm writing this book for you is because this is the book I needed five years ago, when I was manically manifesting and attracting abundance into my life that stressed me out and which didn't end up working out – and why? Firstly, it wasn't meant for me and secondly, it wasn't my soul's aligned abundance. When I was setting intentions I wasn't actually being very intentional; I held high expectations of myself and my desires; I was controlling. I was yearning to manifest the love I wanted and the career success, but I was looking in all the wrong places and operating from a deeply unregulated nervous system and body. All of which meant the results I got in the outer world were matching my inner reality and limited beliefs.

Now, my life looks completely different, as does my manifestation practice. I've managed to heal my hormonal imbalances and finally show my body and nervous system how to relax, slow down and release the trauma of the past. This isn't a race, so make sure to go slow with your own body as you're healing. It's time to come home back to your body, Queen, and make peace with it and with your nervous system. It's been protecting you all this time and now it's time to reclaim your power and manifest through alignment and ease. To help with this, you can balance your chakras, too.

Chakras and the Nervous System

Surrounding our physical body, we have our energetic field, which is a few centimetres away from the physical body and includes the aura and the chakras.

There are seven main chakras within our energetic body (which exists a few inches outside of our physical body). These can become blocked, stagnant, underactive or overactive, so ideally you want all of your chakras open and balanced to create internal harmony and balance in both your body and your nervous system.

In fact, some of the main chakra positions bear an extraordinarily close resemblance to the nervous system itself, leading many to believe the two are connected. The crown chakra is most commonly associated with the overall nervous system, so this is a great chakra to work with if you want to start regulating your nervous system and bring the body into balance. I would also recommend working with your root chakra, as this can become unbalanced when there is anxiety and stress in the body (see the Aligned Actions at the end of this chapter for ways to do this).

Crown (purple)

Third Eye (indigo)

Throat (blue)

Heart (green)

Solar Plexus (yellow)

Sacral (orange)

Root (red)

The location of the seven chakras in the physical body

Balancing your chakras will help to take you a step closer to connecting with the core energy of your desire and aligned abundance.

The Core Energy of Your Desire

I want to wrap up this powerful chapter on the nervous system and alignment by introducing you briefly to one of my favourite techniques, which will help you to release expectations, become magnetic and calm your nervous system. The core energy of your desire is the true pure essence of your desire – free from your human expectations and control. I'm going to go into how to connect to the core energy of your desire later in the book and how I discovered this life-changing technique, so I don't want to spoil it for you now, but I do want to share with you why this connects to the nervous system.

Aligned abundance will bring you peace and relax your nervous system. By connecting to the core energy of your desire, you connect to the true source of creation (the Universe) and to the purity of your desire. Working with the core energy of your desire when manifesting helps you to bring it into your aura and energetic field, and then into the body to bring it into fruition (embodiment).

In connecting to the core energy of your desire through your aura, you also connect to your desire free from limiting beliefs, fears and resistance, and your nervous system will already know this soul desire well. This is why many people say they feel calm and peaceful around the core energy of their desire. You'll then be able to work with both the core energy of your desire and your nervous system to make aligned decisions when it comes to your manifestation, all of which will help you to recognize aligned abundance when it comes flowing into your life.

Aligned Actions

Action

Using the chakra guide opposite, I want you to work with each chakra and the colour of that chakra to identify if there are any imbalances in these energy points. As mentioned, the crown chakra is associated with the overall nervous system, but work with each chakra one at a time and see what comes up.

You can balance your chakras through meditation, and you can find one on my YouTube channel that you can listen to for free (search for "Align Your Energy and Chakras Meditation Emma Mumford"). You can also balance your chakras through wearing clothes and eating foods that represent the colour of the chosen chakra. I personally love to work with crystals that represent the individual chakras and to invite in their energy through adding suitably coloured plants to my garden or buying decor for my home in the colours of the chakras.

See which chakra you feel most drawn to. Notice where you feel the most shifts and how you feel when wearing and eating food that's the colour of a particular chakra; for example, does it feeling calming to your body and nervous system?

Intention

Reflect on your biggest takeaways from this chapter and commit to slowing down and balancing your nervous system. This week, commit to trying one or a couple of the somatic suggestions in this chapter to support and love your nervous system. In the long term, aim to integrate these techniques into your daily or weekly practice and ensure you have enough space and time in your schedule to go slow and nurture your nervous system.

Journaling Prompts

- Does my nervous system feel calm and balanced or stressed and anxious?
- Does this desire/decision feel calming to my nervous system?
- Does it feel safe to have my desire?
- Do I have enough space and slowness in my life for my body to relax?
- Where do I feel tension or stress in my body?
- What can I do this week to start regulating my nervous system?

ALIGNED REFLECTIONS

- Manifestation is mind, body, spirit experience, so to bring our desires into reality we have to bring them into the body. If you're feeling unregulated, anxious or overwhelmed, what effect do you think this will have on manifesting your desires?
- Being able to operate from a regulated and grounded space when manifesting is vital to ensure you're setting aligned intentions that will enable you to receive a flow of aligned abundance.
- The nervous system determines whether our manifestations are lasting or fleeting.
- If you've been struggling to take aligned action or make aligned decisions toward your desires, chances are your nervous system doesn't currently feel safe holding that desire.
- When you can bring balance into the nervous system, you can start to make aligned decisions and choices from your intuition rather than emotion.
- When you're in space of an unregulated energy, you're setting intentions fuelled by emotions and are manifesting through your limiting beliefs, fears and trauma.
- The longer we avoid our emotions, the longer they'll sit in our energy field and body and can eventually manifest into our reality.
- Manifesting is all about energy and emotion is energy in motion, meaning manifestation is an emotional experience and we tap into our emotions to create our reality both consciously and unconsciously.
- If manifesting is stressing you out and causing you anxiety then look at where you may need to reset and support your nervous system so you can realign in a way that creates sustainability, consistency and an environment where your body can thrive.
- Work on the inner world and you'll see how your nervous system starts to relax and trusts that your abundance *is* safe to receive.
- You'll know it's meant for you by the way it feels.

Declutter Your Energy and Life

Now that you're starting to create shifts, manifest miracles and lean into a state of inner and outer regulation, it's time to create the space for aligned abundance to flow into your life. Creating the space for aligned abundance is a mind, body, spirit experience that I break down into physical, emotional and spiritual decluttering. Just like the energy in our home needs a good cleanse and shift about every now and again to allow new energy to flow in, this goes for your spiritual practice and your own energy field, too! While there's a big focus on physically decluttering in the manifestation world, and rightly so, very few speak about the benefits of energetically decluttering your mind of the past and also your energy field of any stuck or stagnant energy.

I've been a lover of feng shui for many years and often share the importance of decluttering your life to welcome in new abundance and energy. For me, this is a seasonal practice that I have committed to for over seven years, during which I've seen huge shifts from this alone. I make the commitment to declutter my life of anything no longer serving me every spring and autumn equinox, and summer and winter solstice (the turning points of the seasons, which you'll learn more about in chapter 10, "Manifest with Nature"), and to welcome in new energy as we enter a new season.

It's become such a habit for me that we now have a running joke in my Manifestation Membership about how much new money we manifest when we declutter as a group. That's the power of decluttering: you can literally manifest money out of nowhere! I challenged one of my good friends Kaitlyn to do this and she manifested finding £1,000 that'd been tucked away in a drawer! Now, I don't tend to go around leaving money in drawers, so I personally haven't manifested anything quite like that. However, I have manifested new opportunities, sales and wins through decluttering mentally, spiritually and emotionally. The great thing about decluttering is it doesn't just have to be money that you manifest when decluttering your garage; it could even create the space for something like your dream relationship to manifest in your life. Don't underestimate the power of cleansing your home and your life!

Decluttering Equals Abundance

So why does decluttering your life equal abundance? The National Soap and Detergent Association shared a study that showed decluttering can cut down 40 per cent of the average home's housework. More importantly, it leads to a reduction in the stress associated with a disorganized living space. All of which goes to show that purging anything that isn't alignment with you anymore, or "clutter", serves as a pathway to a more serene and clear-headed state of mind.

I don't know about you, but when I have a Sunday reset by cleaning and organizing my space, I'm like a new woman afterwards. If I have a clear and flowing space, I know I'm more likely to feel positive, productive and calm in my surroundings, as opposed to stressed and distracted when my working or living space is full of clutter or mess. In a more spiritual sense, by cleansing anything from your life that's no longer serving you, you come into alignment with who you are here and now. You align with the version of yourself who has your desire and you create the space for new abundance to flow in.

A great example of this would be if you were to spot a lamp that you really wanted to buy for your living room, but you already have a worn and dusty lamp that's been there for years and there isn't any other space to put a new lamp, as clutter and furniture cover the floor. Where could you put the new lamp if there's no space? By decluttering your living room of the old lamp and any other items that are in the way, you now have the space for that bright new shiny lamp you've been so excited about buying. And how would you get to enjoy the lamp anyway if it were hidden behind clutter? It can't even get into the room. In the same way, how can you expect your desires to get into the energetic room (your energy field) if there's no space?

Last year as I turned 30, I went through a big shift in my life as I entered a new decade and cleansed so much from my life. I wasn't happy with my wardrobe and, despite my quarterly cleanses, I still had clothes I hadn't worn for years. I kept telling myself things like, "But you loved that top when you were 23 and you might fit into it again one day!" Or, "I know I don't wear these colours and haven't worn this in three years but I might want to again." I was resisting the identity changes that had taken place for me, including in my body.

This time around I was brutal, and anything that hadn't been worn for a couple of years went. If it didn't suit the colour palette or style of who I was now, it got donated. A great question that I asked myself when clearing out my closet was: "Does this represent me here and now in this year?" Whenever I asked myself this, I got real honest and could easily answer yes or no. What happened was I that I got even clearer around my new and improved style, and guess what? As a result, I had the space in my wardrobe to buy the clothes that represented myself now. Today, when I open my wardrobe, I feel expansive, inspired and always have enough clothes, because I'm prioritizing the energy of me here and now, not something I wore seven years ago in a totally different season of my life!

Just to be clear, this isn't about me encouraging you to donate your whole wardrobe or buy a ton of new clothes. Alignment isn't about fast fashion or encouraging you to upgrade your possessions every season. Nowadays my decluttering looks minimal, as I do it so often and have found my groove and style with it. But I did need a good purge in the beginning, because although I love being organized, I used to keep hold of a lot of things back when I first spiritually awakened. I remember taking a photo of my first declutter and it covering nearly half of my living room!

As humans, we accumulate a lot of stuff and our homes, work spaces and even cars can hold on to a lot of stuck and stagnant energy if we're not regularly creating flow. If you want to see an example of flow in your home, choose a room and just move around a piece of furniture or an ornament or two. You don't need to declutter, simply to dust or shift around a few items and then see how the energy in the room has transformed just from that one small change.

The Energy Behind Spring Cleaning

According to a recent survey conducted by waste removal experts HIPPO, over half of British people have rooms in their homes that are unusable due to clutter, despite most of us feeling badly about it. Fortunately, these statistics also point to spring as the most likely opportunity for decluttering to take place, with almost 40 per cent of UK adults claiming they'd clear the clutter as part of a spring clean.

The reason behind spring being a turning point for many people when it comes to cleaning and decluttering is because the equinox and start of the new astrological year both fall within a week of one another at this time of the year. I will go into these energies in more depth in chapter 10, "Manifest with Nature", but essentially the spring equinox and the new astrological year signify new beginnings, new energy and a time when we shed the heavy layers of winter and welcome in the new. This is why many of us feel the pull to clean and declutter around these astrological turning points, as even without knowing about their significance, we have an urge to let go and welcome in a new season in springtime.

For some of you, the thought of decluttering your home or a room might feel completely overwhelming, especially if you haven't done this before. The secret is to start off small, pick a room, a corner or even just one drawer and set a timer. I normally give myself an hour and see how much I can get done. This is much more expansive for me than feeling the dread of tackling the whole house at once. If you feel motivated and want to dedicate a day to decluttering and organizing your home – great! If not, take it room by room and commit to doing one room a week or a month. If you can time it with the seasonal changes of the equinoxes and solstices, that's brilliant, as the energies around these sacred events support decluttering and welcoming in the new.

The reason why we can feel this shift so powerfully in our home and work space is because these places are where we usually spend most of our time. Just like our home when we don't have regular clear-outs, we can become stuck emotionally and energetically, and stagnant in our mindset and in our energy field. This means that the flow of abundance can slow down, as we're less likely to reach flow state (see chapter 14) when we're in a stagnant or cluttered vibration. This is also when any negative thoughts or past limiting beliefs can once again take up space and energy in our mind. Just like your home, your mind, emotions and energy field all need a good declutter every now and again to release what no longer serves you and create the space for new abundance, energy and positive emotions to flow in.

Let's take a look now at some different types of decluttering.

Physical Decluttering

Physical decluttering means sorting through and organizing your physical environment, which could include your home, work space, car, garage or garden. Think about where you spend most time and the physical spaces around you where your energy accumulates. This can include items, clothing and possessions, too – anything in your physical surroundings! It could also look like evaluating your job, for example, and decluttering your career if that no longer feels in alignment. Are there any tasks you need to get done, such as booking a hygienist appointment at the dentist, taking the dog to the groomer, or cleaning your car? Although these are more like general tasks than decluttering, you're still creating space in your life by decluttering any stuck or stagnant chores you've been putting off.

Examples of physical decluttering: cleaning, tidying, organizing physical spaces you spend most of your time in. Sorting through, getting rid or donating items, such as clothing and possessions. Anything you've been putting off completing in the physical, including health and beauty.

Top tips

- Make your decluttering manageable and start off with just a room or an area, and set a timer for the job.
- Hold an item for three seconds and see how much joy it sparks within you and the space you're in. (This is a tip from the organizational Queen Marie Kondo and I highly recommend reading her books if you want to learn more about how to declutter your physical space.)
- Ask yourself if each item reflects you here and now: does it feel in alignment still?

- Give thanks to the items you've chosen to let go of for all they've given you; then donate or sell them to a new loving home. This helps to avoid waste and creating more stuck and stagnant energy in Mother Earth.

Emotional Decluttering

To declutter ourselves emotionally, we need to turn to our inner world and reflect upon our inner work, emotions, limiting beliefs, fears and even trauma. All of these take up space in our mind and in our energy, so if they are ready to be released it's time to declutter them! However, you can't force the inner work to come up, nor do you need to. Your mind, body and spirit will always know the right time to bring up any inner work gently and the suggestions here are simply to release what no longer serves you. As you may already know, when we hold on to old emotions, pain or fears, the body keeps the score. Those emotions stay within us and impact our manifestations, reactions and habits. So doing a regular emotional declutter is the key to alignment and manifesting regularly.

Examples of emotional decluttering: inner work and releasing any stuck or stagnant limiting beliefs, fears or trauma from the past. Releasing trapped emotions through your physical body. Processing your emotions and feelings and letting these move through you during activities such as yoga, dancing, running, shaking, screaming or any other way you feel called to. Regulating your nervous system and releasing anything that is causing you stress or tension as much as possible.

Top tips

- Look at any stuck or stagnant emotions within your body and use tools like EFT (Emotional Freedom Technique) to tap out the energy and release emotions.
- Journal and reflect upon any thoughts or feelings that have been coming up for you.
- Keep a dream journal and note down any emotions or messages that come up, as often these are messages from the emotions within your subconscious mind.
- Lovingly identify and release any limiting beliefs blocks that are holding you back. My third book, *Hurt, Healing, Healed*, is the perfect book for this and will also help you to install new positive beliefs.

- Reflect on your relationships in your life, including family, friendships, romantic love and your relationship with yourself. Is there anything you can declutter from these relationships in your life? Have you clung on to a friendship longer than you needed to out of fear? You don't need to cut people off or declutter them for good, but if you do need to create some space or honour your feelings, this is a great way to release any uncomfortable situations in your relationships. We can hold so much stuck and stagnant emotions and energy in all of our relationships.

Spiritual Decluttering

Spiritual decluttering looks like focusing on your energetic body, including your aura, energy field, spiritual practices and spiritual being as a whole.

Examples of spiritual decluttering: cleansing your energetic body, the aura and energy field of any stuck or stagnant energy. Decluttering journals, notebooks, manifestation boxes, vision boards and anywhere you store your spiritual work and reflections. Spiritually decluttering can also look like decluttering your past-life triggers and emotions, manifestations and inner work.

Top tips

- Reflect on your spiritual practice and declutter anything that no longer serves you or feels unaligned. Look at your daily rituals or practices for manifesting or raising your vibration: do these still feel expansive and uplifting? Change your meditation practice, routine or manifestation practice if it feels like a chore or needs some new energy injected into it.
- Revisit your manifestations, any manifestation boxes or vision boards, etc., and release anything that no longer feels in alignment or that you don't want to manifest anymore. You can always upgrade these, so take some time to sit with each one and decide whether you want to upgrade it or release it fully. You can release manifestations by burning or destroying the paper they're written on in a way that feels right to you, or simply declare to the Universe that you no longer want to manifest this and affirm what you do want to manifest instead.

- Get rid of any journals or notebooks with inner work, gratitude or spiritual practices from the past. We very often keep these for sentimental reasons. I do keep the odd gratitude journal from certain moments in my life, but on the whole I get rid of journals and notebooks to release the energy in them, as you'll be surprised how much this accumulates when pouring your emotions and soul onto the pages. If you have a designated inner work journal, make sure to burn or destroy this once you've finished with it to release the emotions for good.
- Surprisingly, our past lives can also contribute to this life's clutter! If you've found yourself diving into past-life work and some lessons or triggers have been coming up for you, work to integrate and release these with a past-life regression practitioner.
- Give your energetic body, aura and energy field a good declutter by cleansing. You could do this with an aura spray, ethically sourced white sage and palo santo, local sage or with crystals. With any of these tools, direct the spray or smoke around you, starting from the top of your head and all the way down to the soles of your feet. Affirm as you're doing this that you are releasing any stuck or stagnant energy and any energy that isn't yours to carry. See this moving through you and into the ground below your feet to be cleared and transmuted by Mother Earth. It's a good idea to do this practice regularly or when you feel you need to clear your energy.

* * *

Decluttering is a great way to create the space for new energy and to start to let go of what's no longer serving you. I want to take you deeper into your own energy now and share other ways you can release old or stagnant energy to up-level your vibration and align with your desired reality.

Overwhelm

A common block that I see when it comes to manifesting and a reason why people fall off the manifesting bandwagon is down to feeling overwhelmed. This impacts their consistency with both their rituals and their energy, which in turn creates inconsistency with the results and desired feelings.

If you're feeling overwhelmed or overstimulated then some decluttering needs to happen. What bad habits have you picked up recently? Have you been ignoring your practices? Have you been going to bed later than usual? It's common when we feel overwhelmed to slip into behaviours that distract us, and which temporarily help us to cope and feel comforting – but these habits may not be the best for us in the long run, and may mean you're neglecting the things that are important to you and where you really want to put your energy. Where are you emotionally overwhelmed in your life? If you've been experiencing a particularly triggering or emotional time of late, make sure you give yourself the space to process and allow these feelings to be released.

Look at your daily routines and rituals – are they serving you? How can you make your daily practice more manageable and expansive? For example, many believe that in order to do a full gratitude practice, you must write down 10 points of gratitude every morning. However, for me, this was the quickest way to kill my gratitude practice as it didn't feel aligned and it ended up feeling like a chore. Now, I simply write down three or five points of gratitude each morning and after all these years, these still enable me to be consistent, happy and full of gratitude each morning. Keep in mind that it's *your* manifestation practice, so as long as it feels good to you that's all that matters. Strip your practice back to the basics and connect to the practices and rituals that feel exciting and expansive to you.

Remember, less is more when it comes to manifesting, so it's never about how much you're doing or how many times you've done a practice; it all comes down to your energy and vibration. Don't clutter your energy field and mind with practices that don't feel good – we don't have time for that! We only have time for practices and rituals that feel aligned and that bring us closer to joy and our desire.

Balance

Alignment essentially means balance, and creating balance in your life invites alignment in. Now, while you can certainly set the intention to be balanced in all areas of your life, this doesn't mean you're exempt from life. Life will still happen and it's important to check in with yourself regularly and notice when you feel out of alignment or unbalanced. Maybe you want to revisit your work–life balance? Or maybe you want more balance in your downtime to create the space for creative projects? Maybe you're even experiencing an imbalance in your body or hormones and your body is highlighting where more balance is needed. Maybe balance for you in this season of your life looks like slowing down and going inward, instead of busying yourself constantly and rushing around.

What balance looks like will change from season to season, so make it a regular habit to sit down and evaluate whether you feel balance in your life and where you may need to create more. Balance allows your energy to be balanced and receptive, making you the ultimate receiver and magnet when it comes to abundance. Just like in the manifesting process, we go 50 per cent of the way. Everything in the manifestation process is about balance and giving and receiving in equal measure. So when we apply this divine balance in the Universe to our daily life and habits, we become an energetic match for receiving and co-creation. Very often in the manifesting process we do too much through control and fear, so making sure that you feel balance in your life will reflect this energy into your outer experiences and manifestations too.

Create Shifts and Changes

As we've explored already, decluttering your life and energy creates the opportunity for change and shifts in your life by making the space for wonderful, new aligned abundance to flow your way. As we also explored in chapter 3, "Create a Shift and Miracle", we create these powerful shifts in our life through transforming how we view things. Decluttering any thoughts, feelings or situations that no longer serve us will help us to create powerful shifts and changes. For example, if you've been hanging on to a relationship which you know doesn't feel good anymore, this will be all taking up space in your energy and life where an even more aligned and abundant relationship could come in if there was room for it.

We block the flow of abundance by holding on to people, places and situations that aren't in alignment with us anymore. As I mentioned earlier, this doesn't mean you to have to cut people off or move halfway across the world – unless you really want to. But really evaluate how you are spending your time and who with. Are your current home and location bringing you closer to your desire, or have you been putting off following your dreams of living elsewhere out of fear or convenience?

If you want to create a shift or change in your life you must make the first move, as once you create the space the Universe will deliver up-levelled and more aligned opportunities and choices to fill the space you've created. Imagine it like a vacuum: you create the space and the Universe must fill the energy vacuum you've created with aligned abundance. If you're saying no to anything that no longer serves you and you're focusing your energy on your desired reality, the Universe has no option but to bring people, places and opportunities that align with your new vibration and focus.

Check in and Pivot

Every quarter, usually on the turning points of the seasons (these being the spring and autumn equinoxes and the summer and winter solstices), I will check in with my manifestation box and my vision board. I like to do this every three months, to make sure that my desires still feel in alignment with me and that they still feel good. In the past, I've sometimes gone years without looking at my vision board and have then felt disheartened that certain things weren't manifesting, when in fact it was either down to me not putting energy toward these desires but forgetting about them instead, or because I simply didn't want to manifest them anymore. Having desires in your manifestation box or on your vision board that aren't in alignment with who you are here and now only takes up space energetically and creates stuck and stagnant energy.

So I invite you to sit down with your journals, boxes or vision boards and reflect on your manifestations; go through each manifestation and ask yourself, "Does my desire still feel in alignment with me here and now?" If the answer is "Yes" then great! Keep going and spend some intentional time with your desire and give energy to it regularly. If your answer was "No" then you can either choose something new to manifest or up-level your desire if you feel it's up-levelled and grown with you. If it's easy enough to remove it from your manifestation box or vision board then do so, but if you feel okay with it still being on there then honour what feels good to you. If you decide you now want something different, declaring to the Universe that you "clear, cancel and transmute" this manifestation is enough in itself. The Universe knows you are choosing differently through your intention and will get to work on the up-levelled or new desire.

Discover Alignment

Every three months, again on the turning points of the seasons, or as and when I feel intuitively I need to, I'll use locally sourced sage or aura spray to cleanse my home and energy field. I spoke about how to do this in the spiritually decluttering tips above, and it's also a good energy hygiene practice with which to reset your energy and clear out any stuck or stagnant energy from the previous season.

Hopefully, as we've journeyed through the power of decluttering your energy and life, you can see how impactful these practices and rituals can be in creating space in your life and welcoming in the new. When I want to come back into alignment with myself or align with a new season of my life I always turn to these decluttering practices I've shared with you and see HUGE results from this. I want to end this chapter by sharing some examples with you from my community and how the power of decluttering has transformed these wonderful people's lives ...

"I spent a large part of 2023 decluttering financially. Decluttering negative thought patterns, decluttering my home, to reflect the feelings I would have in my dream home. I had a goal of 50k by February 2024. I knew I also had to take inspired action but decluttered while cleaning and had energetic letting-go rituals throughout the year. From January to February 2024 I achieved multiple manifestations I had set out to achieve as big steps. I took inspired action by paying off a big tax bill in January, then on 31 January I got a call to say I was being gifted £50k by family ... I had only said to my husband the week before, 'I would love a holiday, a trip to Majorca would be great' – as well as my money manifestations, which he knew I was working on! We were also gifted this in the same week. You honestly couldn't write it!"

Rebecca D, Manifestation Membership Queen

"Decluttering my physical space declutters my mind, I think clearer and have more clarity. Many times, I have had abundance come to me out of nowhere. My work space needed an overhaul and once I did that, I was presented with two separate paid opportunities to work with people in a wellbeing capacity on top of my own job, neither of which were even on my radar, and I have future opportunities for more of this type of work.

On decluttering my home space recently I found things I'd completely forgotten about and sold them on for £40. It goes to show, when you clear out the baggage it leaves you space to receive so much more."

Sandy W, Manifestation Membership Queen

"I had to go back for a smear test after a year due to a HPV reading and it took me five months from the reminder to go. I was worried about the outcome. At the same time, I was asked to do some admin for a family member for his business – again, something I felt I had to say yes to and didn't want to do! I did both of these finally in the same week and felt such a pressure lifted. I was then asked to apply for a role which would be a promotion at work and was successful, with a pay increase of more than I expected! I also became much clearer on some goals at this point and just have a real sense of flow and ease at the moment – not linked to health or my work! I have no idea how it's all linked but I'm no longer ignoring anything that's playing on my mind and just getting it down."

Toni E, Queen from my Instagram community

Aligned Actions

Action

Go through the tips and suggestions from this chapter on how to physically, emotionally and spiritually declutter your home and life. Choose some suggestions and tips that feel good to you from each section and action these. Make a commitment over the coming weeks or months to declutter your home and work space fully, and donate, get rid of or sell anything that no longer feels in alignment. Set a timer if needs be and focus on one area or room if this will help to break up the task.

Intention

Revisit any vision boards, manifestation boxes or journals where you store your current manifestations. Reflect on each one and see whether these still feel in alignment in the here and now. Up-level any that you have outgrown, or release them if you feel called to remove and let them go fully. You can burn or destroy in a way that feels good to you anything that you want to release fully. Set new intentions if you feel called to. Also set a reminder to spend time with your intentions and to do this reflection ritual every three months if you can.

Journaling Prompts

- Does my desire still feel in alignment with me here and now? (Go *through each desire*.)
- What do I need to declutter and let go of in my life?
- What areas in my home or life feel stagnant or out of alignment currently?
- What tips to declutter physically, spiritually or emotionally do I feel called to try?

ALIGNED REFLECTIONS

- Just like our home, when we don't have regular clear-outs emotionally and energetically we can become stuck and stagnant in our mindset and energy field.
- When we hold on to old emotions, pain or fears, the body keeps the score. Those emotions stay within us and impact our manifestations, reactions and habits. So doing a regular emotional declutter is the key to alignment and manifesting regularly.
- Remember, less is more when it comes to manifesting, so it's never about how much you're doing or how many times you've done a practice – it all comes down to your energy and vibration.
- Everything in the manifestation process is about balance and giving and receiving in equal measure.
- We block the flow of abundance by holding on to people, places and situations that aren't in alignment with us anymore.
- Imagine it like a vacuum: you create the space and the Universe must fill that energy vacuum you've created with aligned abundance.
- If you're saying no to anything that's no longer serving you and focusing your energy on your desired reality, the Universe has no option but to bring people, places and opportunities that align with your new vibration and focus.

Release Expectations and Control

As humans, we're designed to take control of and to place expectations upon life. These expectations form when we're children, when society and our parents/caregivers place their own expectations on us about our lives, and they continue through our education all the way into our adulthood, with our partners' expectations of us and ours of them. In our adult years, we then form expectations around our own life, whether this is about how old we want to be when we meet the person we marry, whether to have children or not, or where on the career ladder we want to be by the age of 30. We place expectations, too, on our bodies and how they should look at various ages. We may also create expectations about exactly when our manifestations should materialize. It's safe to say control and expectations are there for all of us – even for me as a seasoned manifestor and author.

It was only when I turned 30 that I knew my theme for this new decade of my life was to release my expectations and allow the Universe to show me where I needed to be. As this journey unfolded I documented it on my podcast, and I discovered how often expectations came up for me around friendships, people pleasing and about what I expected of myself. "Expectations" became the buzz word of my year as I dove deeper into why my twenties had felt like a heap of unfulfilled expectations in some ways, yet also the most wonderful abundance and success I could ever have imagined possible.

How We Get in Our Own Way and Control

When we try to force and control our manifestations, we're saying to the Universe, "I don't trust that you've got this, so don't worry, I'll micromanage everything to make sure it happens." You then start to place expectations on the hows, the whens, the ifs and the buts. Which are all not in our control. Feeling the need to control is a very human reaction to feeling unsafe and not being able to trust yourself and the Universe. This is why it's essential to set intentions from a place of regulation and work on your relationship with trust and the Universe (see chapter 8, "Trust the Universe").

Forcing and controlling are both restrictive energies that stop us from experiencing the pure joy, expansion and flow available to us in the manifesting journey and in life in general. Think about the version of yourself who has your desire or dream life: would they be checking their inbox for an email about that promotion 30 times a day? Would they be micromanaging every detail or would they be enjoying their desire? Remember, manifestation is a co-creation process and we only ever need to go halfway to meet the Universe. It's then our job to surrender, let go and receive.

Manifesting a Specific Person

When it comes to our relationships, this is a great place to highlight issues around control and expectations. I get asked often, "Can we manifest an ex back or a specific person?" Having been there myself very early on in my manifesting journey, I came to realize just how disempowering some teachings are around manifesting your ex back and that they're also not coming from a space of aligned abundance. At the time, I really wanted my own ex back, but as I reflect on that now from the healthiest and happiest relationship I've ever been in, I know I wasn't fully in my power or manifesting from an empowered and aligned space back then. That's not to say everyone's journey will look like mine, I have seen people get back with their exes, but I'd encourage you to dive deeper into why you want to manifest that person back into your life and how they're showing up currently. Remember that you can't date someone's potential, only who they are here and now.

I also see this not working for many people because of the control and expectations they place on the Universe to manifest that specific person. While being clear on what you want in a relationship does help the manifesting process, holding the Universe to ransom about one person is only ever going to block you and create more lack. Being open to all possibilities is being open to ALL possibilities. When we surrender and let go, we're saying, "This or something better for the highest good of all." You don't want to manifest something that isn't in alignment with you or that will bring you challenges or unhappiness. This is why it's key, even when manifesting a specific person, to remember that the Universe can see the whole plan for your life and the bigger picture, so trust in the highest good and manifest the most aligned abundance that brings you true happiness – whoever that may be. If you do want to manifest a specific person, I suggest focusing instead on how you want the relationship to feel and keep open to all possibilities of who that could be. What is for you can never pass you by.

Drop the Pressure

True alignment means manifesting for the fun of it, not because you want or need something. Manifesting should be the cherry on top of the cake of your already happy and fulfilled life. When we manifest from a space of lack or think that our desires will bring us an emotion or feeling, we set ourselves up with those expectations that very quickly lead us down a path of more lack and nonfulfillment. Your manifestations won't give you anything: you must give yourself whatever it is you seek first, so that you're always manifesting from a space of alignment, flow and nonattachment.

A great example I want to share with you is about how I dropped my expectations around work. Previously, I'd held high expectations for myself and the intakes I'd get with my memberships and courses. Notice I said expectations and not goals or intentions? I'd been trying to smash through an income glass ceiling, but not matter what inner work I did, I kept seeing small consistent growth but not the reality I really wanted to experience. So I decided to release my expectations and knew that whoever was meant to join in that intake was aligned.

What happened next blew every expectation I'd previously had out of the water: I doubled my membership when my goal was only half that number. Attendance on my courses also doubled as more people started discovering my work. All because I let go of my control, expectations and allowed the Universe to deliver what was really meant for me – which was so much more! Our expectations can limit us, so if you're forcing £10,000 to manifest, for example, when the Universe actually wants you to have £100,000, you'll end up blocking this with your expectations, disappointments and not opening up to all possibilities.

But HOW will it Happen?!

My number one tip for getting in your own way and blocking your aligned abundance is by focusing on the "hows". This conversation comes up time and time again in my work and my simple answer is: it's not your job to know how your manifestation will happen. During my manifesting journey, I can confirm pretty much all of my biggest desires haven't happened in the way I thought they would, but in even more incredible ways than I could comprehend! The "hows" are not for us to worry about; that's the Universe's job. It's your job to align and receive.

Very often people with fixed incomes will say, "There is literally no way money can come to me when I'm on a fixed salary that doesn't really go up." Or, "The only way I can manifest money will be through winning the lottery ..." Nope and nope! If you believe you have a fixed income that can't increase – guess what, you're right! And if you believe that money can only come to you through the lottery – then guess what, you're right again! When you can release your expectations and control around how your desire will come to you, you open up to all possibilities, because there really are infinite possibilities for how money and abundance can flow to you.

In one of my Instagram Q&As recently, I was asked, "Can you really manifest winning the lottery, or is it luck?" After sharing my answer on this and how the person needed to open up to all possibilities without trying to control things by focusing on the lottery, another follower responded saying it was possible, as they'd won £100,000 on premium bonds last year and were also on a fixed income.

I always love to bring in the Law of Oneness here: what is possible for one is possible for all. As it stands, over 7,200 people have become millionaires through the UK lottery since 1994, winning over £94 billion in prizes. So that is over 7,200 REAL examples of how winning the lottery is possible. Many get disheartened when they see others manifesting what they want to achieve – so flip this with the Law of Oneness. The reason why you're seeing so many people around you announce their pregnancies when you're trying to manifest getting pregnant, for example, or people going away to your dream holiday destination is because you are a vibrational match to this and your desire is much closer than you think. If you weren't a vibrational match or it wasn't close, you simply wouldn't be seeing these things as often as you are. So when you see others manifesting your desires, get excited – because this means your desire is close!

Today, try for one moment to commit to dropping the hows and remember that no matter how much planning, controlling or placing expectations on the Universe you do, your desire is most likely going to happen in a way you haven't even thought about yet and that gets to be exciting! Stop fighting the flow of the Universe by trying to predict how your desire might happen; allow yourself to be surprised by the Universe and step out of your own way. It doesn't matter how your desire comes to you, really; all that matters is that you get to experience your desire and that you're happy, thriving and feeling amazing about it. So trust that the Universe knows exactly how to achieve just this!

What is Your Why?

Another way I believe I manifested the above big business shifts, was by taking the focus off the end result or releasing any vanity around numbers or money, and by focusing on my "why". Why did I want that many people in my membership? I also turned my focus to the value I was giving and making sure the value and content in my membership and courses reflected my why: my values and my desire to help people and give them the best resources and results. If we don't know our why, our manifestations simply become materialistic rather than having a deeper meaning and purpose.

I very often hear people say they want to have a six-figure business, yet when I ask them why they sometimes struggle to answer, or really know what that level of income actually reflects. It's not the money you want – we never actually want money – it's what that money represents for us. For me, it represents freedom and the ability to live life on my own terms. You don't want a six-figure business that burns you out, that feels like hard work and is full of unaligned clients. What you actually do want is a business that feels easy, that never feels like work, that rewards you generously, that gives you financial freedom and choice, that is full of your dream clients, with an aligned team helping and supporting you, and that adds incredible value into the world and helps lots of people. Dig deep into the why of your manifestations and what the external desire actually represents and its value.

This is another great reminder to ask yourself: "How does my desire positively impact the collective?" Manifestation is not just about what we can get out of our manifestations but the impact they have on other people and how they can help others. How can you manifesting a large sum of money or your dream relationship positively impact the collective too?

Watch Out for Self-Sabotage

When we're feeling in alignment and happy, why do we sabotage ourselves? Self-sabotage doesn't just happen when we feel out of alignment; we can still self-sabotage in moments of happiness and flow. The reason why we self-sabotage is to keep ourselves safe. It's also why you see people win the lottery and then blow everything within a few years. While they are a vibrational match for the win, their money beliefs don't match the new level of money they've obtained, so out of fear they'll find any way to blow the money to feel safe and comfortable again. When we look deeper into control and expectations, we can very often find self-sabotage close by; although we may feel happy and be manifesting abundance, that doesn't stop our subconscious mind from feeling unsafe, our body unregulated and so fear starts to creep in – reinforcing the control and expectations placed on yourself or others.

Look at how you may be self-sabotaging through control and expectation: do you ever feel disappointed when someone does something for you, or do your manifestations never quite hit the spot? Or when things are going smoothly, do you instantly fear something bad will happen because all is going well? There are many ways self-sabotage can creep in, but you'll often find it rearing its head during the second step of the manifesting process, "believe", and when you manifest your desires. Look at what inner work may be coming up for you and what is making you feel unsafe when holding and sustaining your desires. If you realize that some inner work may be coming up for you around self-sabotage, I would highly recommend visiting my book *Hurt, Healing, Healed* to help you identity and release this limiting belief.

Hold and Sustain your Desires

In a recent Q&A I was asked, "How do I hold and sustain my desire?" This is a topic I covered in *Hurt, Healing, Healed*, but it's just as relevant here when it comes to releasing expectations and control. It's one thing manifesting your desires, but you actually want to keep them and see them thrive, too! While you can be an energetic match to your desire (a bit like the lottery win example above), this doesn't automatically mean you will hold and sustain your desire if your identities and beliefs don't match this new up-levelled season of your life.

As an example of this, when I was manifesting my dream man back in 2016, I did manifest the "dream man" for that season of my life and the person I was then. However, I was unable to sustain this relationship due to my own trauma and the inner work that was coming up for me; hence why I started self-sabotaging and becoming out of alignment with this person. Nevertheless, I do believe everything happens for a reason and now that I'm with my fiancé I know why that split had to happen. I also admit I wasn't showing up as my best self in that relationship in a way that could sustain it.

Whatever your own desires are about, are you able to show up as your best self in your manifestations right now? Just like a relationship, your manifestations need to be nurtured and loved too, so that they can thrive and you're able to enjoy them fully in your life. Your desires deserve all of you, your incredible energy and the love you have to give – they deserve the best version of you. Now, this isn't to scare anyone or to make you fear losing your desires; it's more about getting honest with yourself and making sure you're in the best place to hold and sustain your desire before it arrives, so you can focus on enjoying the moment and the aligned abundance that you truly deserve!

Going against the Norm

It's also okay to do things differently with manifesting. If we start to place expectations and control on our desires, it's sometimes because we're projecting someone else's success or journey onto them while thinking we'll get the same result. While you can use other people's successes as great inspiration, often the path to your own success will look very different. Everyone's alignment and versions of success will look different and that's why it's so important to stay true to yourself and what feels in alignment for you. Make sure you're not projecting societal expectations onto your desires, or that other people in your life aren't controlling your dreams and what they should look like.

As an ex-people pleaser, I know how much pressure I used to put on myself to control my desires, so that they'd conform to everyone else's expectations of me and my life. I also used to place huge pressure on myself to be successful and create the life I wanted to give my inner child, which she never had when I was small. But this only ever led to more expectations and control, and the sense that I didn't trust the Universe to look after me. Everyone's journey will look different, so don't compare your day 1 to someone's day 743, how it should look, or the timeframe or timeline, for example; the timing will be perfect for you and mean you receive exactly what is meant for you in the most aligned way.

Navigate Seasons of Feeling Out of Alignment

There will be phases in your life when, no matter what you do, the alignment just isn't quite there. Just because we have the power to create our realities, this doesn't mean we're exempt from life. Life still happens to every single one of us.

I know from writing this book and going on my own aligned abundance journey over the last three years that those seasons when I've felt out of alignment and couldn't reach alignment, no matter what I did, all served a purpose and passed eventually. It was in those moments of feeling lost, helpless and frustrated that I learned the most valuable lessons about the energy I needed to step into and who I was meant to become in that season of my life. Sitting in the uncomfortableness allowed me to align authentically in a cyclical way that has enabled me to be able to walk my talk and write this book.

So yes, there will be times you don't feel in alignment, but actually you're aligned with exactly where you're meant to be. This is once again releasing our expectations and control around how we should be feeling or where we should be. When you release the pressure and need to be in alignment you're able to naturally align moment to moment with exactly what this season is teaching you.

So whether you don't feel in alignment with where you're living right now and there isn't an easy fix, or you're locked into a contract at work and can't just magically align with the job you do want – whatever your situation, trust that alignment can be found in this season. While it may look different to how you've been envisioning your aligned abundance throughout this book so far, know that feeling good is accessible to you here and now, and it's in this surrendered space that true alignment and miracles can flow in your life. This too shall pass.

Tap back into Joy

Joy is the ultimate creator and, when we feel happy and joyful, we don't feel the need to control as our energy is focused elsewhere. We only tend to try to control things when we feel lack and frustration around not having our desire. True alignment means listening to your body, going with the flow and not forcing or resisting. I'll cover this in more detail in chapter 14, but for now I just want to share with you how releasing our expectations and control allows us to tap back into joy.

Joy is such a freeing and light energy, whereas control and expectation are lower and denser energies or vibrations, meaning that when we're in that place of controlling we're zapping all the joy out of our desire and our day-to-day life. We start to notice the lack, notice the hole where our desire should be, and then we try to control some more to bring back the joy.

The only way you can tap back into joy is by releasing the shackles of expectations and control and by saying "f*** it", quite literally! It's time to enjoy your current view, get grateful, surrender and know that no matter how much controlling you do, it'll only ever zap your joy and peace. Lean into those activities and things that bring you joy in life. Use them as a positive distraction and somewhere to focus your energy. A great affirmation I created during these moments that really helped me shift so much is:

My capacity for joy grows every day. Today, I feel even more joyful.

Look for those glimmers and moments of joy in your life, as when you focus on them they'll continue to grow until joy becomes a regular experience and vibration for you.

Joy is often found in the small things, so don't underestimate how much joy you can tap into just by playing with your children or pet, or by helping a stranger, for example. Gratitude is also the quickest way back into the energy of joy, so look around you now and count how many things you can be grateful for. Joy can only be felt in the present moment where control and expectation can't be felt. Those emotions can only ever be felt in the past or in the future, so bring yourself back to the present moment and ground yourself into the joy accessible to you here and now.

Review Your Relationship with Receiving

Finally, to wrap up this chapter ... oh, this one is a biggie! What is your relationship like with receiving? If you aren't very good at receiving help, support, gifts, love and compliments, how can you expect to be a good receiver of aligned abundance?

If you're a controller like I used to be, then you can guarantee that you're the one who tries to make things happen! Why wait for the Universe when you can be the one to deliver it more effectively and quicker! Well, how's that been working out for you so far? If you're like me in the past, probably not all that well. Now, that's not to say I didn't manifest during this time; of course I did, as we are always manifesting. My level of control and surrender toward other desires was naturally different, too. But when it came to the real big desires that I wanted, I just kept hitting block after block and rejection after rejection – all because I was sat in the driving seat, not knowing the route and certainly not letting the Universe guide me.

When we're open to receiving in all areas of our life, we become an aligned receiver and the more that we allow ourselves to receive compliments, gifts, money, love, hugs – whatever it is – the more we flow into the vibration and energy of receiving. Remember that like attracts like, so the more you open up to receiving, the more abundance you receive! That's not to say no action is required; you can't just sit around expecting to win the lottery just by being open to receive: you still have to buy the ticket. But if you're someone who struggles with receiving like I did, then I can guarantee you're currently blocking your level of joy and abundance in your life.

I believe that our level of alignment is a direct reflection of the level of joy in our life and that being open to receiving allows you to tap into the joy and flow the Universe wants to bring your way. Although being a giver and supporter is a wonderful trait to have, everything needs to be in balance – including giving and receiving.

Women are very often the caregivers and supporters for many people in their lives, so I find that their relationship with receiving is often unbalanced or completely depleted. Of course, anyone can have an unbalanced relationship with receiving as we all have different blocks and beliefs, but if you are a woman then know this is very common and that the balanced divine feminine energy is the ultimate receiver! Society teaches women that we must work hard and be providers, givers and play into the divine masculine energy more (we all have both the divine masculine and divine feminine energies within us). This is often the starting point for an unhealthy relationship with receiving.

I also believe blocks around receiving come down to self-worth and trust. For me, it came down to both of these: I didn't trust the Universe to support me or show up for me and I had people-pleasing tendencies from childhood wounding that made me want to give to everyone around me to avoid the feeling of loss again. I also couldn't trust the masculine after abuse in my childhood and adult relationships, so of course I become the hyper-independent woman who thought she didn't need to receive.

Healing my relationship around receiving shifted so much for me. Nowadays, I'm the ultimate receiver: work feels so much easier as I work less and attract more; my relationship with my fiancé is balanced and I easily receive all forms of support and love from him; I no longer feel weird when receiving gifts at Christmas and on birthdays; and the level of abundance I receive is more now that I am an aligned magnet and receive all the abundance that the Universe wants to bring into my life.

So how do you heal your relationship with receiving? I will go into the trust and self-worth aspect of this in chapter 7, but it all starts with intention. Today, I want you to open up to receiving by placing your hands on your heart space (in the centre of your chest) and repeat the below mantra:

I am open to receiving more aligned abundance and support.

Universe, show me how good it gets to be.

For the next 24 hours, note down all the receiving opportunities that come up for you – for example, whether a loved one offers to lend you a hand, a friend buys you a coffee, or you unexpectedly win a competition. Jot down whatever examples of aligned receiving come your way and how it feels to receive each once.

If you find yourself going to say, "Oh no, I'll get this", or, "Are you sure? I don't mind doing it", then stop yourself and allow yourself in that moment to divinely receive. Over time it will become easier and easier to say, "Thank you, that would be great" and to relax into receiving all kinds of abundance in your life. It's all about building your receiving muscle and being open to receiving just 10 per cent more each day. When you become an open and aligned receiver, manifesting abundance will become an effortless and regular experience!

Aligned Actions

Action

Open up to receiving more by asking a loved one or a friend to plan a date or day out so you can receive; they must plan everything from the location to the food, and not let you know what they're planning. This will take some surrendering on your part but have fun and allow yourself to fully receive! We did this in my Manifestation Membership and people saw huge shifts in their abundance mindset just from doing this action alone. If you don't have someone you can ask to do this for you, plan a receiving date for yourself where you book a service like a massage, for example, and fully receive during that date with yourself. Explore if any resistance comes up with this. You can let the other person know why you're asking them to do this for you, if that would help.

Intention

A great mantra to use in moments of control is:

I release any stress or tension in my body and the need to control.

I hand over my expectations to the divine and trust the Universe to deliver my desire in the most aligned way and in the right time for the highest good of all.

I let go of the need to control and relax into receiving.

This is the perfect intention for when you catch yourself worrying about the hows or trying to control your manifestations. Write down a list of your previous manifestations and how you *thought* they'd manifest. Underneath this, write down how they actually manifested and how this differed to your visualizations or expectations. It's important to remember that your desires will likely happen in a way you haven't even thought about yet, and having this list in front of you will help you to relax into surrendering the hows and see from your experiences that there really are infinite ways that aligned abundance can come to you.

You can also use my "Releasing Expectations and Control" meditation, which will assist you with this intention and with releasing any fears or pressure you're carrying. You can find the meditation in the resources for this book at www.emmamumford.co.uk/alignedabundance.

Journaling Prompts

- Why am I manifesting this? (Go *through each of your biggest goals and desires.*)
- How does my manifestation positively impact the collective? (Go *through each of your biggest goals and desires.*)
- How can I open myself up to receiving 10 per cent more today?
- How would I describe my relationship with receiving in the areas of money, compliments, love, gifts, support, etc. (Go *through each area and explore how you feel receiving in it.*)
- How can I reclaim my power and give and receive in equal measure?
- What expectations do I hold around myself and my manifestations?
- How can I release these expectations and surrender to the unknown?

ALIGNED REFLECTIONS

- When we force and control our manifestations we're saying to the Universe, "I don't trust that you've got this, so I'll micromanage everything."
- Forcing and controlling are both restrictive energies that stop us from experiencing the pure joy, expansion and flow available to us in the manifesting journey.
- Remember that manifestation is a co-creation process and we only ever need to go halfway. It is then our job to surrender, let go and receive.
- True alignment means manifesting for the fun of it, not because you want or need it. Manifesting should be a cherry on top of the cake.
- You must give yourself whatever it is you seek first so that you're always manifesting from a space of alignment, flow and nonattachment.
- The "hows" are not for us to worry about; that is the Universe's job. It's our job to align and receive.
- The reason why you're seeing so many loved ones announce their pregnancies if you're trying to manifest getting pregnant, or people going away to your dream holiday destination, is because you are a vibrational match for this and your desire is closer than you think.
- Dig deep into the "why" of your manifestations and what the external desire actually represents.
- Your desires deserve all of you, your incredible energy and the love you have to give – they deserve the best version of you.
- Everyone's journey will look different, so don't compare your day 1 to someone's day 743. The timing will be perfect for you to receive exactly what is meant for you in the most aligned way.
- Feeling good is accessible to you even here and now, and it's in that surrendered space that true alignment and miracles can flow in your life. This too shall pass.
- Look for glimmers and moments of joy in your life; when you focus on these, they will continue to grow, until joy becomes a regular vibration for you.
- When you become an open and aligned receiver, manifesting abundance will become effortless!

Get to Know Your Authentic Self

It's been said, "You don't manifest what you want, you manifest who you are." We all wear a variety of different identities throughout our lives, whether it's the good girl, the independent one, or the one shaped by trauma, or whatever identity we've gotten accustomed to. Our society loves to put us in boxes and neatly label us with expectations around those. In this chapter I want to dive into how identities can sometimes limit us, but also be such an amazing tool for manifesting your wildest desires. (I've put a lot of tools and modalities at the end of this chapter, as this is one of the only inner work chapters in the book – and it's an important one!)

The most common example of an identity which there are lots of societal pressures is that of motherhood. So many women tell me that they initially felt like they'd lost themselves after becoming a mother, when their whole identity was summed up as "Mum". They didn't feel the same anymore and were also not sure of who they were now. So why does this happen? From an energetic perspective, they say your aura completely shatters when you give birth, as you move from the maiden to the mother archetype. Eventually, though, they find their feet again and shift into a new version of themselves.

Although I haven't given birth, releasing my trauma identity made me feel something very similar: things that once brought me joy didn't anymore, I felt different and I couldn't go back to who I was – but I wasn't sure who the new me was either.

My Journey with Identities

"Who am I outside of my trauma?" was the question I asked myself in the depths of my inner work. I had changed and shifted so much over those years of inner work that it felt like getting to know a whole new version of myself. Accepting that my identity had operated from trauma since a very young age was a tough pill to swallow and left me feeling lost, not knowing who I really was outside of trauma. There were periods where I felt lonely, as my friendships shifted and I moved into our lovely home with my fiancé. It was only when I felt at my safest that all of the identities I'd grown fond of started to crumble away.

Nicky Clinch's work resonated with me deeply during this time, especially when I listened to her helping one of my Queens in the Manifestation Membership. Nicky is a Master Maturation facilitator and teacher, and she was coaching members on a live call when she explained, "It's not about forming a new identity, it's about releasing all identities and not needing any." This really got me thinking about my own relationship with identities and why I was so desperate to form a new one.

After I'd worked to release the trauma identity within me (formed from severe childhood trauma and toxic and abusive relationships in my young adulthood), it felt alien to be only getting to know the real me at the age of 30 and to consider why I felt like I hadn't known the real me before now. It was only outside of this and other identities that I could form an aligned picture of who I am at my core, in my soul and in my likes and dislikes. Everything started transforming for me, as my style, my hobbies and friendships changed when I released what was no longer serving me. I felt stripped bare. It felt scary starting all over again with myself, but leaning into what brings me joy has enabled me to soften into needing no identities and allowing the aligned version of myself the peace and life she'd been chasing for so many years.

I realized I was clutching for a new identity because my old ones had kept me safe for all those years – and how could I be mad at my subconscious or nervous system for wanting to protect me? When you release an identity that has kept you safe for a long time, it does feel like you go through a bit of a crisis and ask find yourself asking, "Who am I?" But releasing these limiting identities layer by layer has allowed me to meet myself at level I didn't even know was possible: today, I feel free and, most importantly, aligned. Aligned with my values, my soul and my desires.

These old identities were keeping me stuck for decades despite my already great life and the healing I'd done so far. I was manifesting great things and I was happy, but my old trauma identity was restricting me. It was stopping me from reaching the freedom I truly craved and even the next level of income, for example. Identities can limit us in so many areas, which is why we need to release our need for identities and the ones that are no longer serving us.

Now, there's certainly use to some identities of course – for example, most mothers do want to be known as a "mum", for example – so it's not about taking that away or saying it's wrong. It's just about making sure it's aligned with who you truly are and that you discover who you are at your core in your journey through life. It's about ensuring it doesn't become your whole identity, unless that's the shape that alignment takes for you. On a deeper level, your identities can also include soul traits, how you chose to incarnate and the soul gifts you want express in this lifetime.

Recognize Your Authentic Self

You're more than the sum of all your identities. You are already enough and worthy and deserving of the most incredible abundance as is. Whether it's a trauma identity or a societal identity, no matter what it is, underneath it all lies the true essence of who you are. Your authentic self is who you are at your core, your values, personality and truth, while your conditioned self is shaped by external influences and societal expectations. This is where the real alignment work lies. As I mentioned, to come into alignment with your external world you must first come into alignment within yourself and then with your desire. Coming into alignment with your authentic self involves working with your identities, releasing what no longer serves you and elevating those already within you – the aim is to align with the identity you do want.

One of the biggest questions I get asked in this alignment process is, "What if I don't know who my authentic self is?" Well, right now you may not know what your true self looks like – and that's okay, because little by little you can discover the real you and remove the blocks and layers to expressing your authentic self in the world. Now, it's important to know that you're not being "inauthentic" by not already knowing this self. Due to the many layers of limiting beliefs, fears, trauma and the identities that we carry, few of us actually do know who we are at our core, so it's simply a case of getting to know yourself beneath the layers and masks that most of us wear each day.

A friend of mine, Ema, is a great example of this. She had recently broken up with her boyfriend and told me she didn't like taking up space in life and was aware she didn't allow herself to be vulnerable with others or express her true self. After telling her about the teachings that I'm going be sharing with you in a moment, she messaged me the very next day, saying she had committed to being more vulnerable with her friends and colleagues, and had already received recognition and praise from her boss, which she never usually gets. She felt valued and seen for the first time in her corporate job. This is the power of vulnerability in action! By allowing herself to be seen and express her authentic self, she received aligned abundance in the form of recognition and support in an industry that's not usually known for this.

Time to Meet the True You

Below is the process I shared with my friend for aligning within yourself and getting to meet your authentic self.

Honour your Desires and Needs

Honouring your "yes" and "no" in life is the first step to meeting the real or "new" you. People pleasing will only ever play further into these identities, so only say yes to things when they feel like an aligned hell Yass! and say no when you mean no. Honouring your loving boundaries, decisions and needs will not only heal your inner child (the childlike version of you in your psyche that's with you your entire life), it will show you what you actually like and dislike and what brings you joy.

Shine Your Light

Are you actually an amazing baker but you hide it? Or do you have a deep desire to decorate your home in a certain way but you don't, because of what others would think? Are you shrinking or hiding parts of yourself that make you YOU? Hiding, dimming or shrinking parts of yourself that you love or that bring you joy is stopping you from expressing the real you. Maybe you've always wanted to take up dance lessons, or you're actually hilarious but hide this at work so as to not stand out too much? Look at how your limiting identities may have been stopping you from expressing those quirky, unique and beautiful aspects of yourself. Don't dim your light just to make others feel comfortable.

Get to Know the Real You

Spend time exploring new hobbies and trying new things. Most importantly, give yourself permission to express your authentic self. I even see this around spirituality, when some people feel they need to hide their beliefs or crystals, for example, so they're not judged as being "woo-woo". What makes you happy deserves to be seen by the world and if anyone judges you or makes comments, then that's their problem. I bet you wouldn't mock or belittle someone for expressing their hobbies or passions, would you? So often we fear what others will say or think, when the truth is most of the time people are too busy worrying about their own stuff to care about whatever crystals or books may be in your own home.

Express Yourself

The suggestions above will help you to start gently expressing the authentic version of yourself. But you can go deeper: for example, can you sense anything within yourself that is desiring to be birthed? It could be a book, a painting, a dance or even a song. Expressing the authentic version of yourself looks like expressing your deepest desires and sharing these with the world. So let it all out! You'll also find some journaling prompts at the end of this chapter to help you with this. Expressing yourself also connects to self-image and accepting and loving yourself at your core (soul level) – all your quirks, traits and talents, and seeing yourself as worthy and deserving as is.

Work on Authenticity

Authenticity definitely comes into play when aligning with your true self. As I mentioned earlier, there's no blame or shame here if you notice that you don't always act from a space of authenticity. It may be that you're allowing people to take advantage of your boundaries or that you're hiding your passions or spirituality to keep the peace; or maybe you catch yourself over-exaggerating something and instantly regret this, not knowing where it came from. Look gently at which triggers are present and why you feel you're not operating from a space of authenticity. Be honest with yourself and remember to hold yourself in compassion and love as you witness anything that arises. We are human and no one is perfect. As we align with the authentic version of ourselves, this means removing the layers and masks we've built for protection, but remember that it is safe to be authentic with yourself and others.

Strengthen Your Self-Worth

After progressing through my own identity work over the years, I've realized that the times when I wasn't operating from a place of authenticity or when I was hiding my light or quirky sense of humour were because of my lack of self-worth. The fear of being judged or disliked came up time and time again for me as I unravelled my people-pleasing tendencies. All of the above steps and the tools in this chapter will help you to identify and release people-pleasing habits, which in turn will help you align with your divine self-worth.

Many believe that embodying self-worth is simply about knowing your worth and feeling worthy and deserving of your desires. While that's true, I want to break this down into three pillars of action you can take to strengthen your sense of self-worth:

1. **Practise self-care:** this is about the things we can do each week to show ourselves that we love ourselves; for example, eating well, watching a funny movie, having a relaxing bubble bath and going for a walk.
2. **Express self-love:** this concerns the things we do internally and cognitively to show ourselves we love ourselves; for example, working on your mindset around body image, repeating positive affirmations, and writing a list down of all the reasons why you love yourself. Self-love is all about the relationship you have with yourself.
3. **Embody self-worth:** in order to have a stable and solid foundation of self-worth, we must consistently strengthen both pillars of self-care and self-love. For

example, when I first discovered the importance of working on self-love, I wouldn't be consistent with my self-care and would then wonder why I was people pleasing or making decisions that didn't align with my divine self-worth.

You'll find some videos covering self-worth on my YouTube channel (/EmmaMumford) to help get you started.

Identity Work

The final layer in aligning with your authentic self involves looking at where any limiting identities may be hindering your growth and abundance. However, it's important to remember that there's no right or wrong here in terms of our identities or labels; it's simply what aligns with us here in this season of our life. Limiting identities are shaped by human experiences, often rooted in emotional experiences to trauma. These identities emerge as a protective mechanism, designed to shield us and ensure our sense of safety. We must also realize while we do release the hold these identities have over us, we'll continue to carry these previous versions of ourselves within us. It's a bit like a Russian doll: there's the biggest doll on the outside, which is you now, and inside you have all these other versions of yourself that you've been in the past. Just like a Russian doll, these get smaller and come to have less of an impact on us.

Most importantly, we can get to choose the identities and labels we operate from. For me, this involves simply removing all the labels to these identities and allowing myself to be me, express myself fully and love myself unconditionally no matter what season or identity I'm in. So honour all those previous versions of yourself, because they have got you to where and who you are today and they were doing the best they could with what they knew at the time.

The key to identities and releasing labels is not to cling to any of them; when we remain detached and flowing with how our personality, identities and labels change and evolve over the years, we find peace within this space and a knowing that we are exactly where we're meant to be and who we're meant to be in any moment of time. It's also about removing yourself from any boxes or expectations that have been placed on you or created by yourself as a coping or protective mechanism, so that you can fully express and claim who you're born to be and your highest self. In remaining detached, you reclaim your power and know that no matter what, as long as it feels good and it's in alignment with who you are at your core, that's all that matters. (At the end of the chapter, I've included some journaling prompts to help you dive deeper into exploring your identity and who you want to be in this season of your life.)

Let Go of Your Old Identity

I believe that we meet a new version of ourselves every year that brings fresh opportunities for aligned abundance to flow into our lives, but we may resist letting go of our existing identity because of a perceived fear of loss. When we resist letting go of an old identity, it's usually because it's become familiar and is a safety and coping mechanism for us. To move closer to alignment, there will be some healing work needed around this, in terms of feeling safe enough to let it go and express your authentic self in this season of your life. Reassure your inner child that they're safe and loved and don't need to cling onto this identity anymore. It is safe to let this go and embrace the present moment and self. When you love yourself and have a loving relationship with your true self, everything else will fall into place, as you align and become a magnet to abundance and get into the vibration of receiving your desires.

As we go along our manifestation and identity journey, it's important to check in regularly with yourself and your desires. As I mentioned in chapter 5, it's key to check in every quarter or six months to make sure your desires still align with the version of yourself here and now. After all, we always set intentions from our current mindset, beliefs and energy. This means that over time, as you heal, up-level and step into your authentic self, your desires and manifestations will shift and evolve, too. You may not want to manifest what once were your biggest desires anymore or maybe they've grown and evolved with you!

This also highlights why our desires may not still be in alignment with us. While the Universe is always saying yes to us, if something isn't for our highest good or is out of alignment, it won't manifest. I know when I first started manifesting back in 2016, my idea of my dream relationship was VERY different to what it is now. When I then reset my intentions to manifest my now fiancé, my level of self-worth was hugely different, as were my wants and intentions too.

What I've come to realize is that desires set from a place of unhealed and limiting beliefs or trauma aren't in alignment with our highest self or purpose. While they can still absolutely manifest, as we're always manifesting, these desires will either fall away or up-level. This is why we experience "lessons" and upgrades from the Universe, too. It's all energy; as we up-level so will our desires and experiences. Either the desires in our life up-level and align with us or they fall away. This is not to say everything you've known in your life will start exiting.

While it's exciting to know that my work, relationships, joy and abundance will deepen and expand as I up-level, I've also gone through periods where my friendships have fallen away or people became distant. While this has been a whole grieving process in itself, I can acknowledge how those relationships hadn't been serving me for a while and I was people pleasing or carrying those relationships. What is no longer an energetic match for you is not in alignment and you will align instead with the timeline and experiences that do match your vibration. This is why the inner work is so important along the manifestation journey, so that you can set aligned intentions and receive aligned abundance that feels good to you and your body.

Shift Your Identities to Manifest

So far we've spoken about how our identities can limit our potential for growth and alignment, but we can actually also work with our identities to manifest the very life we desire! This is where the identity work really gets powerful, as you release the old and embody your new desired reality. Once you release the labels and identities that are no longer serving you, you can up-level your current identities to match the new season of life you're in.

You may have heard me say in the past that manifesting is simply about aligning with the version of yourself who has your desire – and that's where identities can help us. When it comes to manifesting your desires, alignment means aligning with the version of yourself that has your desire. Simply put, it's about embodying the identity of that self here and now. This can look like stepping into identities and up-levelling to become the energetic match to receive your desire. Let's use money as an example: what identities would you have if you had your desired amount of money? Or if you had your dream relationship: what identities would you align with? Here are some examples of positive identities in relation to these ideas ...

- money-manifesting Queen
- healed
- abundant
- relaxed and balanced self
- successful entrepreneur
- purposeful self
- mother, wife, girlfriend or father, husband, boyfriend

When setting a big manifestation, I get excited as I know I'm about to go on a journey and become a whole new me to embody this desire. No matter how small the desire, stepping into these new up-levelled identities will create huge shifts and abundance in your life. Some great ways to start stepping into these new identities are by making small shifts over time and by pushing yourself out of your comfort zone by saying yes to opportunities that reflect the new identity you want to embody. When I've manifested my biggest desires, I've noticed it's been a result of me stepping into a new identity and taking action to align with this. We'll be looking at how to do this in chapter 11. For now, I've included some incredible prompts and intentions below to help you start this process and choose these new identities you can align with.

No matter where you are right now, you have the power to release the old identities that have kept you safe and step into a new and up-levelled identity that is experiencing the very abundance and peace you desire.

Aligned Actions

Action

Using the suggestions, tools and journaling prompts given below, I want you to write a list describing the current identities and labels that you hold. Then divide them into which ones feel good and which ones don't feel good and may be keeping you small or protecting you.

Focusing on the identities and labels that don't feel good, I want you to write a letter to them or to your inner child (the younger version of yourself in your psyche) and pour your soul out onto the paper. Go with the flow and allow yourself to express whatever you feel called to write down, including how these have been holding you back or blocking you. Maybe you can even identify where these labels and identities came from or how they've kept you safe?

Once you intuitively feel done with your letter, burn or otherwise destroy or dispose of your list in a safe way that feels good to you. If you can, do this under a full moon as it's a powerful time of release (you can search the dates of the next one online). As you're destroying or burning your letter, imagine these identities and labels being released from you and repeat this mantra:

> Under this full moon, I release the identities and labels that have been holding me back from stepping into my power fully. I reclaim my power and know it is safe for me to release these now and form new and positive identities that serve me. Thank you for protecting me, but I've got this and know I am always protected and deeply loved by the Universe. It is done ...

You can also find my "Releasing Old Identities and Cord Cutting" meditation in the resources for this book at www.emmamumford.co.uk/alignedabundance, where it'll help you to release these old identities energetically and cut any cords or soul contracts to these.

Intention

I'd like you to make notes on the new self or identity you wish to step into by answering the following questions in your journal or notebook. (It might be worth answering the journaling prompts at the end of the chapter beforehand so you feel clearer on your answers.)

- What habits does this new identity require of me?
- What beliefs does this new identity require of me?
- What will my schedule look like with this new identity?
- What boundaries will I have with this new identity?
- What will my self-worth look like with this new identity?
- What will my energy or vibration be with this new identity?
- What will this new identity require me to prioritize?
- How would I describe myself with this new identity?
- Who will I be spending time with regularly?

- What will I do for fun in my new identity?
- Where do I give or invest my energy with this new identity?

If you wish, you can write your answers in the form of a letter from your future self to yourself here today. You may wish to decorate your answers or letter, or even draw the new version of yourself to really take this practice to the next level. I personally suggest storing your answers in your manifestation box or other sacred space so that you can reflect on this scripting often and see it manifest into your reality!

Journaling Prompts

For getting to know the authentic version of yourself

- What are my likes and dislikes?
- What kind of person do I want to step more into?
- What kind of person do I want to be less of?
- How can I step into more of my authentic self, moving forward?
- What do I want to express out into the world?
- Where am I not acting from a place of authenticity?
- How can I implement more loving boundaries?
- How can I start to make more aligned decisions?

For releasing old identities

- Who is my current self and what kind of person am I?
- What labels and identities have been placed on me?
- What identities are my super power?
- Is this who I actually am or this is who I've been told I am my whole life?
- Do I resonate with this label [go through each one] in this season of my life?
- What identities have been keeping me safe?
- Do I want to take it forward with me?

For stepping into new identities

- Who do I want to be in this next chapter?
- Describe who my authentic self or highest self is?
- What traits would I like to turn up within myself that would further help me achieve my goals?
- What energy or word and I'm stepping up and into with

this new identity?

- What identities or traits does the version of myself who has my desire have? (Describe this version of yourself and their habits, boundaries, self-worth etc in as much detail as possible).
- How can I start to embody this new identity now?

ALIGNED REFLECTIONS

- When we align with our authentic self, this means removing the layers and masks we've built for protection. It is safe to be authentic with yourself and others.
- When you work on your mindset around self-love and what blocks you from experiencing unconditional love for self, then you will truly be able to embody aligned self-worth and make decisions from love, not fear.
- There are so many labels that we give ourselves and that society gives us. It's important to remember there is no right or wrong here in terms of identities or labels, it's simply what aligns with you here in this season of your life.
- As we up-level so will our desires and experiences. Either the desires in our life up-level and align with us or they fall away.
- What is no longer an energetic match for you is not in alignment and you will align instead with the timeline and experiences that do match your vibration.
- No matter how small or big the desire, stepping into these new up-levelled identities will create huge shifts and abundance in your life.

Trust the Universe

The saying goes that "what is meant to be yours is already yours". However, your ability to manifest with ease comes down to your level of trust in the Universe and self.

Two of the most common questions I get asked in my work are about this and relate to how to trust the process and that your desires will happen. Trusting and letting go of the outcome have also been two of my own biggest challenges along my manifesting journey. So how do we trust the Universe? And how do we trust in the process? To answer this, I want first of all to take us back to the third step in my five-step manifestation process and dive into this step more in depth.

The Third Step: Trust

This is very similar to the "believe" step in the process, but I think the two are separate. There will be a period where you're still waiting for your manifestation to appear. This is when it's vital to *trust* the Universe's plan and find inner peace with the outcome. Essentially, this means acting like you already have your desire. For example, if you want to manifest your dream partner, you would date yourself, commit to yourself, take inspired action and love yourself. After all, if you had your dream partner, you would *be* relaxed and feeling loved, and getting on with your life. You wouldn't be sitting around waiting on a text, or feeling miserable. So really connect to those feelings you would have if your heart's desire were here right now, and live them now!

To add to this step, take aligned and inspired action. Think about how you can meet the Universe in the field of opportunity and possibility. And remember that this is also the halfway point in the co-creation process, after which you can relax into step four of the manifestation process and let go, before step five: receive.

However, I see so many people getting stuck in this third step whether they are a 90 per cent manifestor or a 10 per cent manifestor, when it comes to the effort they put into the manifestation process. The 90 per cent manifestors are the ones who LOVE to be in control, make their manifestations happen at any cost and who certainly don't feel comfortable receiving. Your 10 per cent manifestors are the ones who'll sit in front of the TV while looking for their dream partner and who are certain they'll win the lottery, yet they don't actually buy a ticket. There are actually some great lessons the 90 per cent manifestors can learn from the 10 per cent manifestors and vice versa. The 90 per cent manifestors can learn more around trust and letting go, while the 10 per cent manifestors can learn more around taking aligned action and meeting the Universe halfway. Whichever type you resonate with most, it's important that both groups align by becoming a 50 per cent partner in the co-creation process with the Universe.

When it comes to trust in the manifestation process this can be broken down into a few areas:

- trust in self
- trust in the Universe
- trust in the process
- trust that it will happen

Over the last nine years of my spiritual journey I've been brought to my knees by the Universe when it comes to trust, and "tested" over and over again until I really embodied and knew what deep divine trust meant. Today, I don't believe the Universe inherently punishes us with "tests", but I do believe we will experience the same karmic lessons or issues in areas we're trying to up-level in again and again until we learn the lesson.

Law of Oneness

So often, we sit in fear and question whether it's for us when others manifest what we desire. In the past when I've felt sad or triggered about someone manifesting something I've been trying to manifest, I would first of all thank the Universe for showing me it's possible. Through the Law of Oneness, we learn that what is possible for one is possible for all. So often we feel that the Universe is "testing" us by shoving others' celebrations in our face, which only highlights the lack we feel in our life. The opposite is actually true: the Universe does not test us and nor does it punish us by seeing others win. It's merely showing you that if they can manifest it, so can you: what is possible for one is possible for all.

I also like to see it as a sign that my desire is near, as if it wasn't in my energy field and within grasping distance, I wouldn't be surrounded by people who share the same desire. Remember, everything comes down to alignment: if you keep seeing people who have what you desire, it means it's in alignment with who you are here and now.

Nevertheless, this can be very triggering, especially for those who want to conceive a child. I had a friend who was struggling to conceive while everyone around her was announcing their pregnancies and inviting her to baby showers. She felt drained from seeing people celebrate while she grieved with every month that brought a period. The good news is that she's now expecting her first baby.

No matter how helpless your situation may seem, as I explained earlier, you wouldn't be in the energy and vibration of the desire if it weren't a match for you. I also believe in viewing these moments as an opportunity to acknowledge any resistance coming up within you. For example, every time I thought I was surrendered in the past, the Universe would put me in the energy of someone around me who did have that desire. At the time, I saw this as a painful reminder of the lack in my life. However, I now look back on and realize these moments were expanders, expanding me into the reality I wanted with this desire. Today, seeing others who've fulfilled the same desire inspires me and reminds me that it's possible and that I, too, could soon be celebrating this manifestation.

Challenge yourself to see others' manifestations as expanders – as an opportunity to expand your energy and experience your desire or what it would feel like before it arrives – and a great way to be around the energy you wish to manifest.

Celebrate with others, get excited and remember what is for you will never pass you by.

Remember the Inner Work

I can recall so many memories over the years where the Universe highlighted to me my lack of trust through my manifestations. Whether it concerned feeling triggered when others manifested my desire, or feeling helpless and like I should give up as it hadn't happened yet for me, one thing I learned along the way was that was no matter how sad I got, feeling sorry for myself didn't help me to manifest things any quicker. Nor did feeling scorned by the Universe. It's important to feel and honour emotions like these and use triggering moments as opportunities to acknowledge the feelings that lie underneath them. Every time I felt helpless I was reminded of the work I still needed to do within myself to develop trust.

The inner work can feel relentless at times and I know how disappointing it can be to hear there's still more inner work to do if the foundation of trust isn't there. You want to achieve your desire, I get it. So why isn't belief alone enough? Why isn't action enough? Developing a rooted relationship in trust will allow these foundations to be grounded: nothing can shake you when your trust in the Universe is unwavering.

Imagine if the Universe granted you your desire but for whatever reason it didn't last. Would you trust something better to come along, or would you fall into the same despair you might feel now that's it not here? As we've seen, a calm nervous system and calm energy are the ultimate magnets for abundance. You can fully enjoy, embrace and experience your aligned abundance when you're coming from a place of trust (that is, love), not fear. That's why the Universe is having you wait – not because it wants you to go through even more inner work just for the fun of it. (There's also the "divine timing" to consider in your trust journey, which I will cover fully in the next chapter.)

It was only when I had exhausted every option, every practice, that I realized I had to "let go and let God". When we release control and put our faith and trust in the unknown, that's when miracles can happen. I also examined my relationship with trust and whether I trusted myself to make decisions, keep myself safe and hold this abundance – and to my shock my answer was "no". Our trust certainly seems to be tested when it comes to our "biggest" desires and the ones we hold the most attachment to, but if you can apply the same level of trust in manifesting a free coffee to manifesting the love of your life, then trust becomes effortless.

Trust and Alignment

Trust goes hand in hand with alignment, as when you trust the process and the unfolding of your life, it's then that alignment can occur. It's only when we tap into alignment that trust feels effortless and easy. For me, this came when manifesting our first home, by which point I had seven years of manifesting experience under my belt and I knew without a doubt the Universe would support me and bring us an incredible house. I also knew that no matter how many times in the past I'd felt like I'd missed out on a manifestation, the Universe only ever subtracts to add something bigger and better into your life. This is why lived experience is so important to draw upon when building your level of trust in the Universe.

A mantra that I repeated almost daily during the house-buying process was:

Somehow and in some way if this house is meant to be ours it will, the money always comes the money is always met.

This mantra dropped into my head during the mortgage application right when I needed it the most.

I'd been self-employed but had turned my business into a limited company a year earlier. Even though I'd been running the business for a total of seven years, when I applied for a mortgage, I discovered that very few banks were willing to lend to companies with fewer than two years of accounts and that the clock resets when you go from being self-employed to a limited company! Given all my hard work and success, I couldn't believe that bettering my business would now impact my borrowing allowance with our mortgage.

Over the course of two weeks, we found one lender who was willing to take into account the projections, salary and annual turnover. However, we still needed to manifest an extra £100,000. It was the tensest fortnight of my life, knowing it all hung on whether the bank would accept the projections. Against all odds we somehow did it, but then came the credit check. Although I knew my credit would be fine, our mortgage advisor told us that they could still lower the amount offered if they didn't like what they found. I kept repeating my mantra multiple times a day to calm my nerves and relax into trust.

I remember the moment Charlotte, our mortgage advisor, rang me and said, "We've done it! You've got the full amount, no questions asked", and the pure joy that washed over me. Charlotte then went on to tell me that in all her years as a mortgage advisor she'd never had a complex case like ours have no questions asked, as the lender almost always come back with further queries. She was in shock and so was I! Through my unwavering trust in the Universe we didn't just manifest the £100,000 extra and a yes, but it happened effortlessly!

Reflecting on this moment of aligned abundance, I put it down to my alignment process and especially the level of trust I finally felt in myself and the Universe. I trusted myself to receive this desire, to hold this abundance and look after it. This manifestation for me was the full embodiment of my trust journey and although we experienced obstacles and fear along the way, the obstacles removed themselves – with no questions asked!

Having read about my journey with trust, I want you to reflect on your desires and ask yourself:

- Do I trust myself to manifest this desire?
- Do I trust myself to receive this desire?
- Do I trust myself to hold and keep this abundance?
- Do I trust myself to look after this abundance?

Take a moment to think about what came up here for you.

Now, if we were to apply these questions to money, for example, trusting yourself to look after the money you manifest could be a big lightbulb moment for you around where some inner work may need to be done if you don't trust yourself to look after the money once it's manifested. The inner always reflects the outer and the level of trust you have with yourself reflects your level of trust in the Universe. If you don't believe you can manifest this desire, how can you believe that the Universe will manifest it into your life either? Feeling safe in your body is so vital in alignment and abundance work, as is knowing it's safe to receive abundance and to hold on to it.

With time, we will see our level of trust naturally build as we build on our lived experiences. Alongside this, we must also look at any blocks that stop us from believing and manifesting our desires. I very often see self-worth come into play when we explore the mindset behind blocks involving trust. I know personally I had a history of things not working out and my trust being broken throughout my life, so why on Earth would I trust myself or the Universe? Through my journey with trust, the Universe showed me my true level of self-worth and why I was manifesting toxic and unhealthy relationships. When I healed my self-worth and realized that I do deserve kind and healthy love, my wants and desires changed too. Over the years my desires up-levelled and I naturally started wanting different things, which is completely normal. The more you up-level and embody your self-worth by removing the blocks to trust, the more aligned abundance you'll effortlessly receive in your life. When I decided and declared what my new level of worth was, my lovely fiancé manifested into my life and the story above is how we manifested our first home together.

Know that You Deserve Abundance

The Universe wants you to see your worth and to know you truly deserve aligned abundance in all areas of your life. But what happens when it all falls apart?

Let me take you back to 2020, the year I had to learn to trust in ways I'd never done before. In 2017, I'd manifested what I thought was my dream relationship. This actually involved my twin flame (a karmic connection between two people), and turned out to be the biggest inner-work initiation of my life. I'd manifested this man with my dream list, he ticked all the boxes and we'd planned a whole life together. Sounds ideal, right? Apart from the fact it was yet another unhealthy, toxic relationship complete with emotional manipulation and abuse.

I was heartbroken and honestly felt like giving up on the Universe, when the rose-tinted glasses came off and I saw what was really happening and how far I'd let my self-worth slip. After all, how could I trust the Universe when I'd gone through three years of on/off empty promises and been diagnosed with PTSD? My nervous system was a wreck, I had hormonal acne all over my body and my reality was anything but a dream. I felt so out of alignment with love and just wanted to be happy.

Like so many of us in 2020, I re-evaluated my life and knew no matter what the psychics said (and yes, they were all telling me this man was meant to be my husband), my happiness and peace were too important. I worked on my self-worth and knew this was not what love looked like; nor did I ever want to experience this again. I also looked at my own toxic habits, as I'd been attracting this to some degree. I was tired of having to piece my life together once again after three very unhealthy relationships in a row.

So I went against what other people were telling me was destined, because I knew I hadn't gone through all I had done in my life to accept that miserable reality as my "fate". I stopped having readings, cut him off for good and fully accepted that I might never meet my person in this lifetime. Still, walking away felt like a huge exercise in trusting the Universe: I had to trust there would be someone else for me and, if not, I'd still be okay. I had to trust that I wouldn't end up in a toxic cycle with someone else, and that I did deserve real love and that this person existed somewhere. I took a big leap of faith into the unknown and, as always, big leaps bring big rewards. Despite what everyone said, I became happy again, I met the most incredible man and, if I hadn't taken that leap, I'd probably still be stuck in that unhappy cycle, hoping things would change.

Trust doesn't always feel comfortable, trust doesn't always feel safe, but when we see the Universe as our divine parent or provider – however it resonates with you – we know that all the Universe wants to do is to provide for us and allow us to experience the most incredible adventures during our time here on Earth. But this must start with you: do you trust yourself to be a divine parent, provider and lover to yourself?

How Can We Regain Trust?

Our past experiences are what stop us from having unwavering trust in the Universe, but as you can see from my story, it's possible to trust yourself and the Universe again. It all begins with trusting yourself, trusting your decisions and trusting your intuition. No matter what happens to us during our lifetime, we're required to trust in the unfolding, trust in the process and trust in our divine parent that anything "taken" from our life will only ever return to us multiplied and upgraded. In all my years of manifesting and teaching manifestation to hundreds of thousands of people across the globe, I've never once had a person come back and say they trusted but the outcome was worse than what'd been removed from their life.

This is why saying "this or something better for the highest good of all" is essential when setting your intentions. You don't want what's not meant for you and you don't need any lessons along the way that aren't for you. Affirming these words ensures you'll always land in the highest timeline for alignment and with the best possible outcome.

Unwavering trust sits at the core of alignment. When I look back at my journey and the countless examples I have from my clients, peers and friends, it's clear that when you divinely trust you step into the portal of alignment and into the field of opportunities that awaits you. Trust is limitless, trust is expansive and trust is woven throughout the fabrics of our Universe – through nature, when we're a baby in our mother's womb, throughout life and even in our passing onto the next life. We are required to trust and trust can be effortless when we surrender and trust in our divine parent, the Universe.

This brings me nicely on to the subject of nature, which we'll cover fully in chapter 10: nature continually reminds us to trust the process and the unfolding of life. Nature trusts that in the depths of autumn, when the leaves fall away in readiness for winter, new energy and even bigger flowers will blossom come the spring. Abundance is always present in nature and it reminds us that there is so much beauty in letting what no longer serves us fall away and trusting in the up-levelling of abundance. As with the passing of the seasons, nature trusts that more abundance is always available.

Avoid Manic Manifesting

Another common block I see around trust concerns "manic manifesting". Manic manifesting is when someone goes from one manifestation to the next without slowing down, or taking the time to enjoy the view and just be present. I also see manic manifesting as being a form of control and a lack of trust. As I described in my second book, *Positively Wealthy*, it was only when I'd manifested everything from my vision board that I realized no matter how much abundance I had, if I didn't address the void within myself I'd just keep wanting more and expecting that to fulfil me.

What about you – are you manic manifesting? Are you gripping on to your desires too tightly? Do you trust you'll be looked after by the Universe? Do you trust that you deserve abundance?

A question I frequently get asked is: "How do I know if I'm a manic manifestor versus ready to receive my desire – what does this look like?" This is one of my favourite questions, because the answer will help you to check in with yourself and be honest about your level of trust.

The simplest way to begin to identify this is to get still. Do this with me now; make sure you're in a quiet space or somewhere you can relax. Turn off any distractions and put your phone away. Start to tune in to your breath, the rise and fall of your chest, your heart beating, and place a hand on your body. Feel the light pressure and touch of your hand.

Now notice what happens when you get still: what comes up? Do you feel calm, peaceful and grounded? What happens in the space you've just created? Go a bit deeper now, listen deeper to the sounds around you – does the stillness continue? Sit in this energy for a few minutes, focusing on your breath and feeling into your body and energy. Then come back to me and continue reading when you feel ready and it feels aligned.

The reason why I got you to do this exercise first is because the body keeps the score, as the famous book by Bessel van der Kolk suggests. Our bodies immediately know when something is amiss and will communicate with us when we take the time to slow down and listen. And it's also about developing your relationship with trust and self. If you're in manic manifesting mode, slowing down like we just did together will have been uncomfortable, heck, even triggering sometimes. Thoughts may have been racing through your mind, maybe you got bored and wanted to skip this part, or maybe fear or doubt started to kick in.

When you're in the "ready to receive energy" step of the manifesting journey, you're quite literally ready to receive! Receiving in multiple forms feels effortless and creating space like we just did feels expansive and peaceful; you trust all is well. You'll know you're in the ready to receive mode by the way it feels. With this in mind, do you recognize you need to build your relationship with trust more? Is there a lack of belief still, despite repeating 100 affirmations? Do you feel impatient about achieving your desire and picking up this book is your last resort before giving up? If so, give up, my love: when we fight the Universe, when we resist, when we control, all we're doing is resisting the flow, ease and peace the Universe wants to deliver. Remember my examples above: I let go, I embraced trust like I had never embraced it before and it paid off big time.

Giving up doesn't mean you don't want your desire anymore or that the Universe will pull the brakes on it; it simply means you're surrendering to support, to guidance and most importantly to trust. It is only when we fall to our knees and "give up" that we allow ourselves to trust fully in the unknown. So how do you build up your trust muscle?

The Two Pillars of Trust

Through learning about trust over the years, I've broken down how to build a solid foundation of trust into the following two pillars:

1. Lived experience

The first way we build trust is through lived experience. If someone has just started to learn about manifestation today, their belief and trust in the Universe will be very different to that of someone who's been manifesting for seven years. Everyone starts at the beginning, but with time and experience you'll naturally build up a level of trust and belief in the process and in the Universe as you see your desires materialize.

Action: Start today by writing down a list of all the times the Universe has supported you and when your manifestations did happen, despite any obstacles, fears or setbacks. Reflect on this list and how impossible it might have felt at the time, or even how much you doubted you'd receive that abundance. Think about how incredible it feels to have this abundance in your life and how your desires always manifest.

2. Mindset

The second way we build trust is through our mindset and belief systems. Having lived experience under your belt will kick-start this process, but your limiting beliefs, fears and trauma will absolutely play a part in determining your level of trust, too. By doing the inner work and using great tools (like those you'll find in my book *Hurt, Healing, Healed*), you can identify and release any negative beliefs that stop you from trusting yourself, the Universe and that unlimited abundance can be yours.

Action: Use the prompts in this chapter to identify whether you trust yourself when making decisions, whether you lack trust in your body and holding your desires (sustaining them) or whether someone has broken your trust in the past and this is why you struggle to trust the Universe (external trust).

Other Ways to Build Trust

As well as working with the two pillars of trust, here are some other ways you can build trust and improve the flow of aligned abundance in your life.

Communicate with the Universe

When you open up a conversation with the Universe, you invite in the opportunity to build trust and build a relationship with your divine parent. Building a relationship with the Universe will help you to know the Universe is there, cheerleading you on the whole way.

Action: Early each morning, take a moment to centre yourself and place a hand on your heart centre in the middle of your chest. Breathe deeply and, on the exhale, say either in your mind or out loud, "Universe, show me how good it gets." If you want to mix it up a bit, set the intention of: "Universe, show me that it's safe to trust today." Both of these intentions will allow the Universe to step in and build trust with you each and every day. In the evening, it might be helpful to note down in your journal what happened throughout the day in response to these intentions to see trust in action.

Read the Signs

Another way to build trust and communicate with the Universe is through signs and synchronicities. You might see repeating angel numbers such as 11:11, 333 or 444, or you may see feathers placed randomly, or even an unusual animal show up, and you intuitively know it's a sign! I love asking for signs and this practice really helped to build up my communication muscle with the Universe. Your angels and spirit guide team are also there to support you and communicate with you as part of the Universe.

Where I feel signs and synchronicities can hinder the trust journey is when you start controlling and using them as an emotional crutch for validation. I can absolutely hold my hands up to this myself and I notice it often in my communities when people ask about their signs. However, no amount of butterflies, numbers or feathers will give you the reassurance that your desire is coming if you don't have a solid foundation of trust within yourself first. So if you're working with signs and synchronicities from a fun and detached energy – great!

But if you start to get disappointed when they don't show up instantly or within that three-hour time limit you set, then the Universe is showing you that you need to establish trust within yourself first.

The same goes for the tarot, oracle cards and psychic readings: if you don't trust yourself, the Universe or the divine plan for your life (more on this in the next chapter), no matter how many people tell you something's meant for you, you won't believe it. All of these divination practices, signs and synchronicities are tools I love using to communicate with the Universe and I recommend them to you, too. Just be mindful of how you're using them and for what purpose. If it starts to feel controlling or you start obsessing, for example, stop using them and use affirmations to communicate with the Universe instead.

Action: If it feels aligned to do so, set an intention with the Universe to see a repeating number, object, animal or whatever comes to mind when you think about what sign you'd like to see to help you build trust in your desire manifesting or the Universe. You could set an intention like this one: "Universe, please show me a pink elephant if my level of trust is building." The more unique the sign the better; try to choose something that would instantly make you think, "Wow, this is undeniably my sign!"

Build on Your Intuition

Trusting your own inner compass is essential when it comes to building trust in the divine plan for your life and the Universe. Remember that your intuition is like a muscle: it must be built up over time and through consistency. So start off small – Rome wasn't built in a day. When making small decisions like your choice of breakfast, purchasing a product or where to go for lunch, tune in to your body. You might notice that one option feels more expansive and lighter, whereas the other feels more constricting or denser. You might feel your body sway in a certain direction or a feel a pull to one option over the other. The secret to building your intuition is through trusting your first initial reaction without questioning it. This is why it's great to test it out on smaller decisions so you get to know your body, your intuitive style and learn to trust those gut feelings and niggles. Then with time, you can start to use this for bigger decisions and know what feels like a hell YASS or a hell no to you. My mantra when it comes to intuition is if it's not a hell

YASS, it's a hell no. If you're ever unsure about a decision, sit with it for a few days and see how it feels to you in two days' time. Allowing the initial fear or emotions to pass through you will help you to tune in again from a more grounded space.

Action: Start testing your intuition muscle by tuning in to your body to make everyday minor decisions. Act on the first gut instinct if that feels like a hell YASS and watch your relationship with your intuition grow. Honour your nos and if you're unsure what the decision is, then sit with it for a while and revisit how you feel in a couple of days' time. Gradually build up to making bigger decisions by getting to know what your yes and no is in your body through feeling and movement.

Start to Feel Safe in your Body

Feeling safe in your body is essential when it comes to manifesting and trusting the Universe (revisit chapter 2 for more on this). Does it feel safe to hold your desire? Small daily practices are essential when it comes to trusting and feeling safe in your body. Work on de-armouring yourself; alongside using the tools and suggestions given here, you can keep reaffirming to your body and subconscious that it is safe to receive, safe to hold abundance and safe to trust yourself.

Action: Start off the morning by placing your hands on your body, one hand on your heart centre and one on your stomach. Breathe deeply into your body and on the exhale release any tension or stress from your body. Then repeat this mantra: "I am safe in my body. It is safe for me to relax and trust myself and the Universe. All is as it should be." As we know, it takes 21 days to change a habit or a thought pattern, so commit to this action for 21 days and document what comes up each morning. Do you feel any resistance to this? Write it all down and see how this shifts for you over the 21 days.

˟ ˟ Aligned Actions ˟ ˟

Action

Pick some of the above actions from the suggestions on pages 113–16 on how to build trust and give these a go. I want you to learn to trust yourself and your decisions, so choose the ones you feel most called to work on and take your time with them.

Trust your body, trust your choices and trust your intuition on what actions feel good to you.

Intention

Reflect on your manifestation journey and write a list in your journal of examples of when you doubted your desire would come, you didn't trust yourself or the Universe, and then what happened as a result. Did you eventually manifest your desire against all odds? What evidence do you have that you can trust yourself to make good decisions and look after your abundance? What evidence do you have that you can trust the divine plan for your life and that the Universe wants to provide endlessly for you?

Journaling Prompts

- What would it feel like to trust 10 per cent more this week?
- Do I trust that the Universe wants to continually provide for me? If not, why not?
- Do I trust myself to manifest this desire?
- Do I trust myself to receive this desire?
- Do I trust myself to hold and keep this abundance?
- Do I trust myself to look after this abundance?

ALIGNED REFLECTIONS

- Remember that everything comes down to alignment, so if you keep seeing people who've received what you desire, this means it's in alignment with who you are here and now.
- It's important to feel and honour your emotions and use these triggering moments as opportunities to witness the feelings that lie beneath them.
- Developing a rooted relationship in trust allows these foundations to be grounded – nothing can shake you when your trust in the Universe is unwavering.
- If you can apply the same level of trust in manifesting a free coffee to manifesting the love of your life, trust will become effortless.

- Trust doesn't always feel comfortable, trust doesn't always feel safe, but when we come to see the Universe as our divine parent or provider, however it resonates with you, we know that all the Universe wants to do is provide for us and allow us to experience the most incredible adventures during our time here on Earth.
- Trust is limitless, trust is expansive and trust is woven throughout the fabrics of our Universe – through nature, when we're a baby in our mother's womb, throughout life and even in our passing onto the next life. We are required to trust and trust can be effortless when we surrender and trust in our divine parent the Universe.
- Just like the seasons, nature trusts that more abundance is always available.
- Give up, my love: when we fight the Universe, when we resist, when we control, all we're doing is resisting the flow, ease and peace the Universe wants to deliver.
- No amount of butterflies, numbers or feathers will give you the reassurance that your desire is coming if you don't have a solid foundation of trust within yourself first.
- If you're ever unsure about a decision, sit with it for a few days and see how it feels to you in two days' time. Allowing the initial fear or emotions to pass through you will enable you to tune in again from a more grounded space.

Alignment versus Divine Timing

Along your manifestation journey, you'll often find there are some manifestations that happen almost instantly, while other "bigger" desires can end up feeling stuck or it's just not the right time! So what exactly is divine timing and how does it impact our manifestations and aligned abundance?

Divine timing is the Universe's timing, which we're not in control of. There's a saying I loved so much that I had it tattooed on me way before I knew about manifesting: "Nothing before it's time." I've always believed in divine timing and that there's a perfect time for everything to happen in your life. Now, as I've grown older and more experienced with manifestation, I see that we may actually sometimes use the concept of divine timing as a kind of waiting room when in fact there is no waiting room in life; life is never on pause. We're either in alignment with something or we're not.

Right Person, Wrong Time?

I love referring to the famous saying "right person, wrong time" when it comes to divine timing. I've often heard famous dating coaches and experts say there's no such thing as "the right person, wrong time", only "wrong person, wrong time". And I'd agree with this; in fact, I would say it applies to all our manifestations, not just relationships. There is no wrong timing in our life because time doesn't exist; it's only here on Earth that we experience time and delays in manifestation. Some people even believe that our past lives, current life and future lives are all happening simultaneously and we can tap into different experiences and timelines using quantum leaping and other quantum techniques.

I'm definitely open to all possibilities when it comes to timelines and everything happening at once. However, again and again I've seen how time can warp, speed up and how we can magnetize our desires to us instantly when we align with the frequency of that reality. My regular psychics have often told me they feel hesitant to give me timelines for predictions as I'm the type of person who can magnetize something to me tomorrow, while others will always have their set timings. The good news is you're now one of those people who can magnetize their desires more quickly too!

I also don't like the saying "right person, wrong time" because it suggests there's a wrong time – and there can't be a wrong time when time doesn't exist and we're always exactly where we're meant to be. It also disempowers people, especially when it comes to love, thinking that the stars will finally align and that somebody will somehow show up differently and magically the relationship will work this time round!

Now of course, there are examples of people meeting and then going their separate ways, only to return years later and have an amazing relationship. Anything is possible, but those people didn't wait for the stars to align, they didn't sit around in the waiting room of life and it certainly wasn't about magic. It was simply part of their alignment process. The truth is that some things are just not meant to be and no amount of "time" will magically align something if it's not meant for you. Very often, what seems like the right thing but at the wrong time may turn out not to be right thing for you at all, and something even better and more aligned for you will come along instead when you least expect it.

Nothing Before It's Time ...?

Let's take it back to my tattoo. When I first heard this quote, I fell in love with it and the idea that everything is divinely timed. Now, nearly 14 years later and knowing about the universal laws, karma and soul contracts, I see things slightly differently.

Soul Contracts

Our soul contracts determine our experiences here on Earth and lessons that we have chosen to embody here on Earth in this lifetime. Some believe that we have "soul meetings" before we incarnate here on Earth to determine what we'll experience, learn and transmute (that is, clear). These soul contracts can include our soul family (the group of people we reincarnate with, which can include our family, lovers, pets, etc.). We can complete and release soul contracts in this lifetime and work through any karma we've come here to resolve. While I believe our soul contracts tend to be set-in-stone agreements, we can put these off if we choose to, which means we experience them at different times in our life or even not at all. Everything is a matter of free will, so we can change the timings of some events in our life. So while soul contracts would determine a divine timing in our life, we do have some choice around this, too.

Free Will

There'll also be events in our life that involve choices made by our own free will and which won't necessarily be about soul contracts. Here on Earth, we have free will when it comes to our lessons, experiences and blessings; we're the creators of our life. Some people question whether manifestation could even exist if everything is predetermined – and that's where free will comes in. We can choose experiences in our life and that's precisely why we can desire certain manifestations, goals and aspirations. While we do have free will, we're also divinely protected by the Universe, which applies to anything that's not for our highest good or that could harm us. Some even say that manifestation comes from our higher self and that we only desire these things because time doesn't exist and we're already experiencing them in the future. I love all of these theories and feel there's room for them all to be true; I also feel we'll never truly know every secret working of the Universe, as that's our job to uncover it in our lifetime – or maybe not at all!

Divine Timing

Which leads me to divine timing – the belief that if we don't have our desire, it's because it's the wrong time. Once again, I feel this disempowers people and only ever keeps them stuck in the waiting room of life. You're not waiting for a bus, Queen. Life is happening now and the future version of yourself already has your desire. If time didn't exist, how differently would you feel toward your desire? Just like my psychic example earlier, if you were told you could manifest it tomorrow, how would you act differently? I see divine timing as meaning divine alignment – and instead of a perfect "timing", I see it as perfect "alignment", where the only delay in the physical world is simply about you aligning with the frequency and energy of your desire.

Divine Redirection

Finally, let's not forget good old divine redirection. We often think that a "no" from the Universe means "not yet". While this is in part true, it's actually a "not this door" from the Universe. Any rejections are simply divine redirections to your aligned abundance. So when you get a no from your dream job, get excited, because that wasn't your door and it isn't your aligned abundance. It's definitely easier said than done when facing rejection, but when you can see this as the Universe clearing out the unaligned opportunities to align your real dream job for you with the higher pay, better location and company car included, you realize the Universe is only ever saying no to bring something bigger and better into your life.

Leave the Waiting Room of In-Between

You're not waiting for the right person, right time; you're aligning with the most high vibrational relationship, job, friend, house, etc., every single day. If someone has said to you, "You'll manifest this when you're 32", for example, it's time to take back your power and know that the Universe can move mountains in your life. You don't need to wait for the Universe to give you a green light and spend your time till then waiting for life to happen. Life is happening now.

A very common block I see when it comes to manifestation is people feeling stuck, blocked, lacking motivation and giving up hope. Please never give up hope as your desire is already yours. Your desire has been planted in your heart for a reason and you are meant to have your desire. Don't see time as a punishment; see it as blessing.

When I was in the waiting room of life before manifesting my now fiancé, I would get so fed up of waiting. I would feel like I was waiting for my life to get started properly. As you can imagine, I felt pretty stuck – until I shifted my mindset into what this "time" was gifting me. I began to realize that one day when this man was here, I wouldn't have all that time for myself; self-care, work and spontaneous holidays with my friends. I wouldn't be in my house anymore and my life would look different, and although the thought excited me, it also made me realize that I'd never be in this season of my life again – and that, actually, I could be really grateful for this time.

Then, when we met and I was "waiting" for us to move in together, I again reframed it into appreciating I wouldn't always have all this freedom of my own space every day and have everything in my home in just my own way, so maybe I could enjoy this season more and not wish it away. Sure enough, time did pass and we did move in together and my life did change in wonderful ways. The reason I'm sharing this with you is because you don't want to look back and think, "Gosh, I wish I'd enjoyed that season more", or, "I wish I could go back to those times and be more grateful." Time always passes and the "in-between" seasons of your life are a blessing too.

Set yourself free from the trap of the waiting room of life. The Universe is not placing you there, waiting to bless you with your desire on 22 February 2026 at 11:32am. The Universe is waiting for you to take aligned action and align with the reality you want to experience. If you're not getting the result you want, then affirm you're getting up and out of the waiting room of life, change your intention, take action and see how this shifts your reality. Remember:

Intention + Action = Desired Outcome

Don't Wait, Take Action

When we're in the in-between stage of manifesting, we usually stop taking action as we feel stuck or are patiently waiting for the next move. But frequently it's us who needs to make the next move.

I'm often asked, "How do you know you've gone 50 per cent of the way and met the Universe halfway?" The simple answer is you've taken your aligned and inspired action and you're now authentically and naturally surrendering and letting go effortlessly. As "Trust" is the third step and "Let Go" is the fourth step of my manifesting process, from a practical point of view, step 3 would be the 50 per cent mark. However, it all comes down to your energy. You'll know intuitively when it's the right time to take a step back, as letting go and surrendering will be as easy as breathing.

If you feel like you're getting frustrated by the wait, remember that your manifestation will always happen when you need it the least. Really, divine timing comes down to you aligning with the right actions and energy to be met halfway by the Universe. I personally see the first three steps of ask, believe and trust as very divine masculine energy steps (action-oriented and driven), whereas the last two steps, let go and receive, feel very divine feminine as you relax into receiving and magnetizing. Seeing the steps in this way can help you to tap into where you need to be focusing your energy.

If you're waiting for a sign, this is it! Don't wait around for the Universe to suddenly bless you one day and decide that it'll be the perfect time to manifest your desire in 167 days' time. Time is not dictating your waiting here; it's your energy and who you are (your beliefs and identities). So even if there was a divine date or time the Universe decides is right for you, you can absolutely magnetize your desires to you more quickly when you take aligned and inspired action. Start by thinking about what aligned action you can take this week toward your desire: is there something you've been putting off that you've been waiting for permission from the Universe to do? Go do it! Get in the field of opportunity and possibility and see what doors and next steps start to open up for you.

Many believe that luck is random, but I believe luck to be intentional and the field of opportunity and possibility that we put ourselves in by taking aligned and inspired action. When you unblock yourself from waiting, you allow yourself to get out there, get to the 50 per cent mark and say, "Hello, Universe, here I am – ready to receive!"

Play with Time

A great way to test time and see how you can bend it is not by finding a Tardis and David Tennant (my favourite Doctor Who), but by playing with the Universe. Very often when "testing" the Universe, you might set a timeframe for when you want to see your sign or receive your manifestation by. Some people can achieve great results with this approach, although I wouldn't always recommend it, only because it can make you hold on to your desire and then feel disappointed if it doesn't happen within that timeframe. The reason why we don't always receive a sign or desire within the timeframes we set is because of attachment. When you're desperately looking out for it and expecting its arrival, you're not in alignment with abundance at all. Yet when you forget all about it and align effortlessly, you'll manifest your desire before you know it!

Time itself isn't as rigid as it might seem. Scientists made a startling discovery back in 2020. They found that, instead of slowing down, the Earth has started to spin faster than at any point in the last 50 years. In fact, the shortest 28 days on record all occurred during 2020, meaning that world timekeepers are considering subtracting a second from our clock because of this change. This means time really is moving quicker and I don't know about you, but from 2020 time seemed to feel really different in comparison to pre-lockdown.

Even though we all experience 24 hours in a day, or 86,400 seconds to be precise, how we define the passing of time is down to us. It's about whether we stagnate and take no action and experience time moving slower, or whether we get out there, have some fun and suddenly notice the whole day has flown by. The key here is joy: when we're tapped into flow and joy, time seems to move more quickly, meaning our desires can flow to us more quickly through the emotional states and frequencies we're vibrating at.

A great way to play with time is to document how time feels to you as you experience different emotional states. For example, does it move quicker when you're feeling more high vibrational and does it move slower when you do nothing or are feeling down? Everything is energy, remember, and you can literally bend time using your emotions, feelings and frequency to align with your highest timeline.

This is essentially what quantum leaping is (a quantum field teaching): jumping into the timeline that has your desire in it. Let's go back to that radio station analogy, about tuning into the radio station (the frequency) that you desire. You don't have to simply wait for your favourite song to be played by the Universe; you change the station and align with the frequency you want to be on. This is how I'm able to manifest things quicker than expected: not because I have a Tardis, but because I take aligned inspired action and align with the timeline that has my desire in it. The more you clear out stuck and stagnant energy, old beliefs and identities, the more you clear the way for you to leap quite literally into your desired reality.

Another great practice I recommend trying is to set an intention for something small like a free coffee and then play with time. See how it feels to set different timeframes around this and what you notice. Do you start looking for it, or does it effortlessly appear more quickly than expected? You may even find some desires appear more quickly than others; this will also help you to identify where you place more expectations or attachment. For example, you might find free coffees manifest for you within a few hours, whereas money could take two days. Playing with time allows you to see that, really, time has no meaning other than as a means to structure our day. When we manifest aligned abundance, we're not waiting for time to pass; we're simply getting into alignment, taking aligned action and seeing how energy trumps time.

Once you've played with this idea, you can start to set intentions like, "Universe, I want to manifest £10,000 through the path of least resistance and in the most aligned effortless way." In this instance you've not set a timeframe, but you've used words such as "path of least resistance", which will help to speed up your desires effortlessly! Tap into words, feelings and emotions when setting your desires and creating affirmations. These emotions and frequencies will help you to see these desires materialize more quickly than you think!

Trust the Timing

You very often hear the words "trust the timing of your life" shared in the manifestation community and I do still believe this to be true, alongside how time doesn't exist. This book is the perfect example of divine timing and how sometimes we can't see the bigger picture. I share the full story of how this book came about later on, in chapter 14, so here I wanted to focus on the timing element.

You see, I had it all planned out that I'd write this book in 2023 once I'd got a publishing deal. Yet the deal wasn't appearing and the structure of the book and inspiration also weren't flowing. I'd written an initial proposal but it was rejected by various publishers. Given the success of my other books and this powerful topic, I couldn't understand why doors kept closing when I knew deep in my soul that this book was needed. Long story short, as I've mentioned, in 2023 we bought our first home and after that some of the deepest inner work came up for me, including what had happened to me as a child.

All summer long I felt lost, shedding so many identities, layers, beliefs, fears and trauma. Every time I tried to write, I couldn't. I had to surrender to the process and trust in the timing. Looking back, I thank my lucky stars I didn't get the book deal at that point in time, as being held to deadlines would have been a nightmare. The Universe knew I had to walk that path before writing this book.

Fast forward to the end of 2023, I felt a surge of new energy toward the book over the New Year and I couldn't stop the flow of words and ideas as I restructured the entire proposal and deleted over 15,000 words. Within two weeks I had my book deal and you'll hear about that divine flow a little later on! I wrote this entire book from scratch again with this new and up-levelled energy, trusting that this flow and alignment made it the perfect time to write the book.

Aligned Seasons

Although time doesn't exist in the Universe, I do believe there are seasons where the Universe protects us and doesn't give us anything we can't handle. I know this book was written in the perfect timeframe because of how it feels and if I'd forced it to happen a year earlier then I certainly wouldn't have been walking my talk with the contents of it! I needed the space and time to heal and embody these lessons before writing the book, so I could hold and sustain the book with ease. However, I didn't just sit and do nothing in that time that passed; I worked on myself and focused on those projects that did feel in alignment and flowed at that point in time.

Remember that you want to be able to hold and sustain your desire with ease, so trust the timing and flow of your life. Right now you might feel called to focus elsewhere, so give your energy there. This doesn't mean you forget about your manifestation; if anything, it will speed it up as you take aligned action in the season you're now in. There's a version of you who is experiencing your desire right now; and it isn't time that separates you from it, only energy. You are that person already and you can tap into this version of yourself here and now by connecting with them.

How are you spending the 86,400 seconds you have in a day? Are you experiencing flow, joy and peace as much as you can in those seconds, or do you currently feel time works against you? There's always enough time for what's important to us when we make the space and prioritize it. Make sure the things you're filling your day with are bringing you closer to your desires and, most importantly, joy. What will you do with your 86,400 seconds tomorrow?

Aligned Actions

Action

Play with time and see how you can make it work for you instead of against you. Step out of the waiting room of life and into aligned and inspired action. The journal prompts below will help give you ideas about what action to take. Set some intentions daily to start testing time (for example, "Universe, I want to manifest a free coffee by 6pm"). See how you feel setting a time limit: does it help you to let go or does it make you clock watch? Once you start seeing your desires manifest, notice which ones flow easier and which areas take more time or don't meet your desired timeframe. Once you've played with time, start playing with words when setting intentions (for example, "Universe, I want to manifest £10,000 through the path of least resistance and in the most aligned effortless way"). What words or emotions speed up time for you and how can you use these in your intention-setting and affirmation process?

Intention

Be intentional with your time and with your manifestations; although you may think this will slow you down, it actually speeds you up! Prioritize what's important to you each day and create the space for intentional practices or time to work on something new, like a project or hobby. Don't let time pass you by; be intentional with each activity in your schedule and challenge yourself to be fully present in these moments. When setting new intentions or even when doing the tasks and actions in this book, set an intention for the time you carve out to do each practice and bring intention into as much as you can throughout the rest of your day. For example, before a meeting, set some intentions about how you'd like it to go; or when brushing your teeth in the morning, think about how you can be more present in that moment.

Journaling Prompts

- If time wasn't an issue what would I do differently?
- Where do I feel in the waiting room of life currently?
- Why does my desire feel stuck: what am I waiting on from the Universe?
- What examples do I have of divine timing working in my favour previously?
- What aligned and inspired action can I take toward my desires?
- What stops me from being intentional with my desires currently?

ALIGNED REFLECTIONS

- We use divine timing as a kind of waiting room, when in fact there is no waiting room in life. We're either in alignment with something or we're not.
- The Universe can move mountains in your life, so don't spend your time waiting for life to happen. Life is happening now.
- Time always passes and the "in-between" seasons of your life are a blessing too.
- If you're not getting the results you want, then affirm that you're getting out of the waiting room of life, change your intention and take action.
- I believe luck to be intentional and the field of opportunity and possibility that we put ourselves in by taking aligned and inspired action.
- The more you clear out stuck stagnant energy, old beliefs and identities, the more you clear the way for you to leap quite literally into your desired reality.
- Tap into words, feelings and emotions when setting your desires and creating affirmations.
- Remember that you want to be able to hold and sustain your desire with ease, so trust the timing and flow of your life.
- There's a version of you who is experiencing your desire right now – it isn't time that separates you from it, only energy. You are that person already and you can tap into this version of yourself here and now.

Manifest with Nature

Have you ever noticed that no matter what happens in the world, no matter how harsh the winter or how many times we as humans overharvest plants and food from Mother Earth, more always grows with time? It reminds me of how in movies about the end of the world, the humans are often long gone but when it's left to its own devices, nature continues to thrive and regrow. No matter what, it seems that nature is always abundant and always replenished – just like aligned abundance within our own life. We only need to look at nature to be reminded of the infinite abundance all around us and available to us.

You may have heard the terms "Mother Earth" and "Father God" before when referring to our divine parents or the Universe. Mother Earth represents the divine feminine energy that we all have within us and gently whispers the energy codes of receiving and abundance. So when we're manifesting with nature, we're being called back to our divine feminine energy and roots.

Although I've been following the seasons and cycles through various spiritual practices since 2020, it was only really in 2023 that I felt the call from Gaia (another name for Mother Earth) to bring more of nature into my work and to surround myself with nature. During the summer of 2023, I took two months off work (which is something I've never been able to do before in my 13 years of being an entrepreneur) and surrounded myself with nature and its healing energy, as I went through my own death and rebirth cycle on entering my thirties. Nature has always had an unspoken power that instantly grounds, relaxes and centres me. It holds so much magic and mystery that I always want to learn more.

Although immersing ourselves in nature can be a deeply healing and a cathartic experience, like it has been for me, we can also work with nature and the seasons to create aligned abundance in our life. Through slowing down, listening and regulating myself with nature, I've learned just how much abundance and our manifestations are influenced by the power of cyclical living and Mother Earth. Here, I'm going to share with you some ways to tap into nature and let aligned abundance flow into your life.

The Wheel of the Year

I first started working with the Celtic Wheel of the Year around five years ago, after hearing various spiritual teachers refer to the equinoxes and solstices and wanting to learn more. The Wheel of the Year is divided into eight festivals that celebrate the turning points of the seasons. These festivals, which have their roots in ancient practices, were revived by modern Pagans in the mid-20th century and have recently become hugely popular, celebrated by spiritual and non-spiritual people all around the world regardless of their religion.

The equinoxes and solstices are solar celebrations (the longest and shortest day and the two points in the year when day and night are equal), while the other four are the Celtic cross quarter festivals that fall midway between these, and include Imbolc, Beltane, Lammas and Samhain. So whereas the four annual seasons are those of spring, summer, autumn and winter, the Wheel of the Year has eight seasons, each with its own festival, energy and frequency that we can tap into to help us manifest our desires.

The Seasonal Energies

Here's a bit more information about each of the eight festivals of the Wheel of the Year and ways to work with their energies to sow the seeds for aligned abundance in your own life.

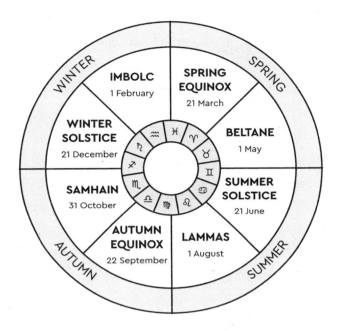

The Wheel of the Year

Winter Solstice (Yule) – 21 or 22 December

Key Themes

- The shortest day of the year and the longest period of night.
- Marks the official start of winter, and the initiation of light returning to the sky as the days start to lengthen, bringing the promise of spring.
- A time for deep reflection, rest, gentleness, releasing and recharging.
- Dive deep, celebrate and refocus your direction for the season to come.
- Set intentions for the next 12 months ahead.
- Winter energy is all about the deep feminine inner journey, making this the season for inner work, healing, shadow work and recuperation before we head into the lighter months.

Rituals

Reflect on the year, what worked well and what you'd like to improve in the New Year, and write this down on a piece of paper. Then invite in the light by lighting a candle. You could then burn your reflective list safely with this candle to let the last year go energetically. Slow down and pause – how can you rest more and be gentler with yourself? The Winter Solstice provides the perfect time to wrap up any loose ends before the end of the year. So if you've been putting anything off, this is your time to take action and create the space for abundance. For example, don't let small tasks or chores dampen your festivities; instead, take action so that you enter into a new year with clear space and energy, not a long to-do list!

Journaling Prompts

- What areas of my life do I need to shine some light on?
- Where do I need to let the light back in?
- How can I slow down and rest?
- How can I celebrate myself this week? (*Action this.*)
- What inner work is coming up for me right now?
- What seeds of beautiful intention can I sow for the next 12 months?
- What am I ready to let go of and leave in this year?

Imbolc – 1 February

Key Themes

- Marks the halfway point between the winter solstice and spring equinox.
- A time to shake off winter, reflect on the wisdom we've gained over winter and plant new seeds of intention ahead of spring. It's also the turning point of the season.
- After months of turning inward during winter, of hibernation and of rest, nature and life are beginning to stir again. You may even start to see the first spring flowers, such as snowdrops.
- This is a time of new life and energy coming into manifestation. You may only be seeing the tiniest hints of shift in your physical reality, but things are really beginning to stir behind the scenes. Just like nature is beginning to awaken after its dormant period, we are

also reawakening with new dreams and exciting plans for the year ahead.

Rituals

Using the journaling prompts below, reflect on the wisdom and insight you've gathered over winter. Think about what is stirring within you now and what areas of your life you feel the light returning to. Make a list of projects and plans you can bring to life over the next few months and plant seeds of intention ahead of spring. You can do this either by writing down Imbolc intentions for spring in a notebook or journal, or by physically planting seeds in your garden. Imagine placing your intentions in the soil with each seed and seeing these bloom with the beautiful plant, come spring.

Journaling Prompts

- What wisdom have I gained over winter?
- How can I begin to shake off winter this week?
- What new seeds of intention can I plant ahead of spring?
- What projects and plans would I like to bring to life over the next few months?

Spring Equinox (Ostara) – 20 or 21 March

Key Themes

- Spring brings in change, shift and positive momentum as we start to see our hard work pay off. You now have the green light from the Universe to start taking action toward your goals.
- Ostara symbolizes a period of birth and renewal. As nature emerges from its winter hibernation, it serves as a reminder of the cyclical nature of life. Now, as day and night become equal in length, this signifies a moment of balance between light and darkness.
- Get ready to ignite your manifestations, because the spring equinox marks an enchanting and abundant time of the year. With the warmth and abundance of spring blossoming around us, it's time to step into the sunlight. Are you ready to plant the seeds of your desires? The spring equinox encourages you to seize this opportunity to set intentions and sow your dreams.

- The spring equinox also marks the start of Aries season (21 March to 19 April), which is the beginning of the new astrological year – the perfect time to set intentions for the year ahead and step into new beginnings and new energy. This creates an incredible time and energy to set powerful intentions for the year ahead. Some people prefer to set their yearly manifestations now instead of in January (the traditional New Year).

Rituals

Spring clean your home and create a shift in your energy and environment by having a good declutter physically, emotionally and spiritually. Start taking action toward your goals and begin creating in whatever way you feel called to. To attract new energy in your life, try something new. Shake off the old astrological year by letting go of anything no longer serving you, cleanse the energy of yourself and your home and set powerful intentions for the coming twelve months. Now that we have the clarity of spring, reflect on any yearly goals you set in January and make sure they still align with you here at the new astrological year. Make sure to get out in nature and feel the winds of change and new beginnings in the air!

Journaling Prompts

- What am I ready to move forward with now?
- What area of my life is the Universe giving me the go-ahead in?
- Where do I need to find balance?
- Where can I connect with joy this spring?
- Do my yearly goals still feel in alignment to me?
- What am I birthing right now?
- What new beginnings are happening at the moment?

Beltane – 1 May

Key Themes

- Marks the halfway point between the spring equinox and summer solstice. The days are now noticeably longer.
- A fire festival, Beltane inspires us to begin to grow into our full potential and bring our dreams into reality! It's a time to reflect on your spring equinox intentions set

six weeks ago and whether what you're doing here and now is helping these come to life.

- Beltane is a great manifesting energy, so get out in nature and feel these seeds of intention from earlier in the year start to bloom now. From now through to the summer solstice marks the peak energy period in the Wheel of the Year for manifestation. So now really is the time to create and bring to life what you desire. As the divine masculine energy returns with summer, we can now see our manifestations come to life.
- A time of fertility, growth, love, joy and sensuality, and sexuality.

Rituals

Call back your power by repeating the mantra: "I reclaim my power and call back all the lost pieces of myself." Connect with nature and the nature elementals (or spirits) as the veil is at its thinnest during Beltane. Beltane is all about celebrating love, so it's a great time to call in romance if you are wanting to manifest a relationship; write a list down of all the qualities and characteristics you'd like in your dream relationship. It's also a great time to do a fire ritual, so create a list of anything you are ready to send to the fire and transmute. This could be the past, emotions, feelings, situations or people you'd like to release. Write down anything you feel called to release and burn this safely, visualizing the fire of Beltane clearing this from you.

Journaling Prompts

- What ignites the fire within me?
- What do I want to create, manifest or birth during these manifestation months?
- How can I fall in love more with myself and life?
- What fire or desire is burning within me right now?
- What do I need to be doing right now to ensure I manifest my desires and reap the rewards come autumn?

Summer Solstice (Litha) – 20 or 21 June

Key Themes

- The summer solstice is the longest day of the year and the shortest night. It's the official start of summer, and of the journeying back to the night as the days shorten, bringing the promise of autumn.

- Traditionally, this is when to celebrate the light, life and ourselves. It's also potent for birthing new energy, new beginnings, manifesting and welcoming in abundance. So now is certainly the time to be welcoming in new energy and your manifestations!
- Summer brings in manifestations, and a time to celebrate the light in your life while ensuring you have balance. It's about calling in your full power to be fully seen.
- It is the sacred season of opportunity and manifestation, and we now experience the most fertile months of the year and see our desires come into fruition over the summer. We're now surrounded by the energy of the divine masculine, so it's perfect time to take action, get out there and see abundance all around you. The summer solstice is a great mid-year point to realign your focuses for the remainder of the year. Check in with your yearly goals and whether they still feel in alignment to you here and now.

Rituals

Celebrate the lighter months by getting out in nature or moving your body in whatever way feels good to you. Celebrate the light in your life and all the things that are going well for you. Also look at what you need to illuminate as you head into the darker months. Write a list of gratitude for all the wonderful things that have come into fruition over the last six months, as this is a great way to celebrate the light and call in more abundance. Spend some time diving deep into this and feeling the gratitude and appreciation for all the blessings you've received so far this year. I'd also suggest writing a celebration list of all the great things you've done over the last six months and making sure to celebrate YOU. It's you who's done the hard work to make all of these wonderful things happen alongside the Universe. Do these rituals outside in nature if you can to take this practice even deeper, as it's great to connect to Mother Earth with the summer solstice and connect to the elementals, the nature spirits, also!

Journaling Prompts

- What am I saying yes to this summer?
- What has my inner fire helped me accomplish this year?

- What three things am I going to bring to life over summer?
- Where can I step into my full power and shine?
- What do I want to fill my life with in the second half of the year?
- Are my yearly goals still in alignment here and now?
- What have I accomplished this year that I feel really proud of?

Lammas – 1 August

Key Themes

- Marks the halfway point between the summer solstice and autumn equinox. Also known as Lughnasadh – a time of the first inner harvest as we begin to see signs of autumn.
- Nature is at its peak abundance, growth and expansion and is ready to be harvested. It's a celebration of creativity, craftsmanship and of harvesting what you sowed earlier in the year. This is a powerful time to connect with your inner abundance and express gratitude for what you've manifested, grown and welcomed into your life throughout the year.
- Lammas celebrates our work for the harvest, and that the intentions and seeds we planted earlier in the year have now come to fruition. It's not only about gratitude for the fertility of the Earth, but also to our former selves for planting seeds, putting in the effort, and knowing how to make our intentions grow.
- Lammas is also a great time to think about where you are heading, and to change course if need be. There's still a lot of time for growth before the winter. Even at the time of Lammas, the trees put on a second flush of leaves. You too still have time for tremendous growth in the coming months.

Rituals

At Lammas, take a moment to feel gratitude for the year so far and the summer season. Write a gratitude list for what you're feeling grateful for in life right now and what abundance has flowed into your life over the last few months. Next, reflect on the last few months in your journal: what has shifted for you? How have you grown? How can you celebrate the abundance now in your life? Think back to the beginning of the year and spring equinox: how have you changed and evolved since this point? Celebrate your growth and overcoming any of the challenges so far from this year.

Journaling Prompts

- In what areas of my life am I currently experiencing great abundance?
- What relationships have helped me to grow and thrive recently?
- What needs most tending to in my life before the season's end?
- What inner growth have I noticed so far over summer?
- What moment of seasonal joy stands out for me from the first half of summer?

Autumn Equinox (Mabon) – 22 or 23 September

Key Themes

- Autumn brings in change, as the leaves teach us how beautiful it is to let things go; it's a time to celebrate all the abundance you've received throughout the year and to look at where to put your focus as we start to retreat inward, into the darker months.
- The autumn equinox is just one of just two moments in the year when the sun is exactly above the equator, meaning the day and night are of equal length. From now, the days will become shorter and nights longer.
- The summer months are all about growth and bringing our endeavours to their fullest potential, while the autumn equinox means taking stock of what we've grown, harvesting it and choosing how to best utilize it, energetically and physically. These changes often prompt adjustments from other areas in our life; for example, is there a new hobby you've been wanting to start but never got round to? Is there a part of your life that you are unsatisfied with? This new season allows us to realign and choose what path we want to take, and even if you're feeling like things are falling away in your life right now, autumn will always be there to remind us change will always arrive – and that there isn't an end to anything, only a new beginning.

Rituals

Write a gratitude and appreciation list for all you've manifested and achieved throughout your year so far. Once you have your list, reflect on each point and give thanks for the "harvest" you've reaped this year so far by reading through each point and repeating, "Thank you, thank you, thank you, Universe, for my heart's desires and wishes you've brought into fruition this year." Take your gratitude even deeper by reflecting on what lessons summer has highlighted for you and what you can give thanks for since the summer solstice.

Next, look at what you need to focus on for the rest of the year to help you achieve your remaining goals. The autumn equinox is a great time to declutter your home and your energy with a good clear out to welcome in change and new energy.

Lastly, it's time to let it all go! Start by lighting a candle and then journaling on the prompt "What can I choose to release and let go of now?" You could write this as a list or a letter and include anything that you feel needs to be released now physically, emotionally or spiritually. Notice what's falling away in your life right now and write it down in your journal. Once you're done, use the flame from your candle to release this. If you're unable to burn your list or letter safely, please destroy in a safe and responsible way to release this from you. As you do so, you can repeat, "I choose to let this fully go now. Thank you, Universe, for supporting me with this."

Journaling Prompts

- What is falling away in my life right now?
- What do I feel called to declutter?
- What blessings and abundance have I received so far this year?
- What seeds of intention do I want to plant for the rest of the year?
- What can I choose to release and let go of now?
- What shift or change am I creating in my life currently?

Samhain – 31 October to 2 November

Key Themes

- Marks the halfway point between the autumn equinox and winter solstice celebrating the end of autumn and brings the first signs of winter. Also known as Halloween or All Hallows Eve.

- A time of deep release, many associate Samhain with death-like energy at the end of the harvest season. It's when we're encouraged to turn inward, rest and regenerate, like the Earth does during the winter months. While it may appear to us that the flowers and trees are dying during this time, deep beneath the soil the Earth is filling its cup and replenishing the soil full of nutrients, ready to birth new beginnings come spring. This is what we too experience as we allow anything no longer serving us to end and die off now.
- It's believed the veil between the Earth and the spirit realm is at its thinnest during this time of year, meaning we can connect to our ancestors, guides and loved ones much more easily during Samhain. Your intuition and inner guidance will also be heightened during this time.
- Although Halloween is typically associated with all things spooky and scary, use this time to reflect on your fears and look at how you can embrace and love the shadow aspects of yourself.

Rituals

Over Samhain, celebrate your past loved ones and ancestors by creating an altar for them; this could include photos, items or even food offerings. Write your loved ones or ancestors a letter expressing your gratitude for them and welcome their energy back into your life. (You can place this on your altar afterwards.) Apples, a sign of life, are closely associated with this festival, so bring them into your home this Samhain – whether you display one on your altar, cook with them or just eat them.

Samhain represents a death-like portal so ask yourself what's dying away in your life right now. Celebrate how far you've come this year, thank the growth, lessons and any shadow work, and let anything die off that is no longer serving you in this season. Also, gently reflect on your relationship with death and rebirth – how can you embrace these cycles? Finally, get out in nature and observe nature going through the process of death and rebirth. Sit with how it is safe to embrace and celebrate the death of cycles and energy in your life.

Journaling Prompts

- What's dying away in my life right now ready to be reborn?
- What am I grieving in my life currently?
- How can I reclaim my magic and transform this winter season?
- What is my relationship with death and rebirth?
- What do I enjoy about the dark time of year? What don't I like about it?

CELEBRATING THE WHEEL OF THE YEAR IN THE SOUTHERN HEMISPHERE

You may also be wondering about whether the northern and southern hemisphere celebrate the same seasonal festivals. The answer is no, the festival dates given here are for the northern hemisphere. If you're in the southern hemisphere you'll be experiencing the opposite season, so please switch the celebrations to match your seasonal turning points.

Honour Your Inner Seasons

As well as the Earth's outer seasons and celebrations, we also have our own inner seasons that impact our energy. Just like the trees and plants, we too naturally go through seasonal changes and cycles, and when we listen to what season of life we're in, we can align ourselves with that energy and use this to magnetize all kinds of aligned abundance to us. However, when we resist it, this is when we may experience frustration that nothing is coming into fruition for us.

Your inner seasons are why you may sometimes have periods of more outward-facing divine masculine energy, where you're manifesting and experiencing new things; while other times you may feel more inward-facing, connected to your emotions and focused on the inner work, with a wintery divine feminine energy surrounding you. You can adapt the descriptions given for the Wheel of the Year to help you navigate the meanings of each of these seasons when you find yourself navigating them.

Cyclical living is another common term used in the spiritual space for working with the seasons, and it means listening to your body and having awareness of the outer seasons, moon cycles, our inner seasons and menstrual seasons if you're someone with a womb. It's an ancient approach to living in harmony with ourselves and nature.

Women and people with wombs will also experience further inner cycles with their menstrual cycle. For me, this next cycle has been a game-changer in terms of how I live my life and where I place my focus around each stage of my cycle every month. I hope that by sharing it, it can help you exercise, eat and live more intuitively with your cycle, too:

Inner spring (follicular stage): This is a time to initiate and begin. You may feel like your energy is coming back at this time and you can start to do regular exercise and movement.

Inner summer (ovulation phase): This is a time to expand and be bold as your energy returns. It's a time to get out there, fully express yourself and have fun.

Inner autumn (luteal phase): This is a time to connect and complete anything you may need to at work or at home. You may feel your energy come down a bit now as you gently head inward, toward your period.

Inner winter (period phase): In this time, as you bleed, it's a great opportunity to reflect and rest. It's also known that during our bleeding phase we are at our most powerful and intuitive, so use this as a time to tune in and connect to your feminine power.

We Too Are Nature

Now, I may have just heaped a whole ton of new information on you about the seasons and inner seasons. But hopefully after reading this chapter, you can see how working with the power of nature can greatly impact our inner alignment and the abundance we experience. They say that there is no greater force than nature, and although this is normally used in reference to destruction, I want to change this story to replenishment and abundance too. Nature is always replenishing itself, providing animals and humans with resources, oxygen, food and water, and showing us the unlimited access we have to abundance of all kinds in this Universe. We have so much to be thankful for when it comes to nature and following its seasons and cycles – because we too are nature.

When we fight against our natural rhythms and cycles, we fall out of alignment, we feel resistance. In the same way, we experience blocks and exhaustion when we fight against the natural rhythms of our body and life. There is a perfect timing for everything in our life and nature shows us just how powerful all parts of the cycle are. Nature has this perfect order of cyclical unfolding and if we remember to connect back into the ancient wisdom held in the world around us, we can align with these sacred rhythms and find peace within these unfolding cycles. Without the rest and inward journey of winter, we would never experience the bloom and abundance of summer, for example. This is the Law of Polarity once again in motion, showing us that the cycles in our energy and in life serve us and our desires greatly.

When we become one with nature and its energy, we begin to flow more in life, we regulate as we honour our seasons and magnetize abundance to us through the portals and seasonal shifts that we have access to. From incorporating the Celtic Wheel of the Year and cyclical living into my life over the last five years, I can honestly say my life has changed hugely for the better and my manifestations flow so much more easily and abundantly as I flow with the season I'm in.

What are Your Manifesting Patterns?

During a powerful live call in my Manifestation Membership with my good friend and peer Vix Maxwell, the creator of New Age Hipster, Vix asked us to reflect on what seasons we tend to manifest the most in and in what seasons we set those intentions. This was a huge epiphany for me, as I realized that I always manifest my biggest desires in spring and set my intentions in winter. Now, of course this falls in line with the traditional themes and timings of the seasons, but there was a whole array of answers, with some members on the call discovering that they set intentions in the spring and manifested them in winter, for example. The important thing was that it helped us get to know our own manifesting patterns.

This brought me so much peace as at the time I was trying to manifest this very book deal. It was November at the time, and I now realized why it wouldn't manifest in the depths of autumn or winter, when spring is my ultimate time to manifest! So that winter, I decided to revisit my manuscript and proposal and made huge aligned upgrades to both that felt SO good.

As if by magic, my publisher, Watkins, reached out again a few weeks later and asked to review the material again. Long story short, within the space of a few weeks what felt like a stagnant situation turned into an aligned situation. Then, on the powerful first new moon of the year, I got offered a deal for the very book you're reading today. So although in this case it actually happened before spring, by releasing my expectations and control over timing, and working with the seasonal energy I was in, aligned abundance quite literally happened!

Another example of this in my life is relationships and moving home. I've met my biggest previous relationships and even my now fiancé around May or June time, and I have always moved home in either April or May. These are big months for me in terms of manifestation and movement – and of course they would be with eclipse season (a big astrological period of destined events and change) happening around this time and the accompanying spring themes.

So just like Vix did on the call, I want to invite you to reflect on your previous manifestations. Can you spot any common themes around when you tend to manifest your biggest desires? Or in what months big change happens for you? Once you can spot these cycles and patterns, you can work even more deeply with nature and the seasons to know when to set your most powerful intentions, take action, release control and surrender to exactly where you need to be.

GIVE BACK TO NATURE

Something that I felt called to do when launching my manifestation course "Attract, Alignment, Abundance", which inspired this book, was to give back to nature to create even more abundance. So I decided that for every Queen who signed up, a tree would be planted in their name. I use an incredible company called Trees for Life that is creating our own grove where we have planted over 300 trees so far. Through the abundance I receive I want to plant even more abundance back into Mother Earth. While this is helping to re-wild the Scottish Highlands, it's also an example of how we can give back to nature and see our abundance create even more abundance in nature.

So think about how you can give back to Mother Earth and create even more abundance in the world, whether that's through planting trees, flowers or even vegetables, doing a beach clean or even looking at your carbon footprint. Looking at how you can give back to Mother Earth and create more abundance only ever creates a cycle of more abundance in your life.

Nature Doesn't Compare

Finally, to wrap up this magical chapter, I want to remind you that while nature reminds us of how abundant we are, it also reminds of us of how worthy we are. In nature, the lemon trees just bloom without anyone telling them to; they bloom when they feel ready to with the whispers of the season's encouragement. Have you ever noticed that flowers don't compare themselves? They simply bloom not caring how big or bright their fellow flowers are next to them, because they know they are worthy and needed. Nature is always teaching us to let go and that actually letting go can be beautiful too, through the gorgeous autumn colours and leaves. If you ever want a reminder of just how beautiful, powerful, abundant and worthy you are, go look at nature. It blooms in all its perfection and imperfection at just the right time and provides unlimited abundance without us even asking.

If you want to see this sort of abundance, just look outside your window or, even better, stand in your garden or outside space. Gaze around at the trees, plants, grass and bushes. Notice how there's an infinite number of blades of grass; do you think you could count them all? Next, look at a bush close by: can you count all the leaves on that bush? Look at a rose or even a picture of a rose if you don't have one close by: can you count all the petals? Finally, on a clear night, look up at the sky and try to count each star; how long do you think it would take you? Nature makes everything freely available to us without conditions – other than that we respect and care for it. Nature is the true definition of infinite abundance.

Next, focus on your breath, take a deep breath in and remember you never have to question your next breath. Your body and the oxygen around you allow you to breathe effortlessly and trust in the abundance of air available to you. Now are you starting to see how truly abundant you are?

When you tune in to nature, come home to yourself and honour your cycles, you create the space for magic to flow to you. Nature is our reminder that there is always enough and that this too shall pass. Each new season brings magic into your life and working with this magic provides beautiful opportunities for growth and aligned abundance.

Aligned Actions

Action

In your journal or notebook, write down a list of your biggest manifestations or abundance and next to each one write down in what month you received them. Notice any patterns that appear and then work out in which month you set these intentions. Once you identify which two seasons you tend to set intentions and receive intentions in the most, work with both of these to supercharge your manifestation process. For example, if it's your pattern to use winter for intention setting, set your intentions during winter; and if it's your pattern to receive abundance in spring, prepare to receive your desires in spring and take action beforehand.

Intention

Follow the Celtic Wheel of the Year and the rituals and prompts in this chapter to help guide you through each season. Set intentions at the turn of each season and work with their energies to bring your desires into fruition. If you haven't done so already, plant seeds of intention for the next three months (the season you're in currently) and watch these come into fruition.

Journaling Prompts

- What inner season of my life do I feel like I'm in currently?
- In which seasons do I tend to manifest the most change or abundance?
- In which seasons do I tend to set my biggest intentions?
- How can I start to connect and work with the seasons?

ALIGNED REFLECTIONS

- We only need to look at nature to be reminded of the infinite abundance all around us and available to us.
- Just like the trees and plants, you too go through changes and cycles with the seasons.
- Summer marks the sacred season of opportunity and manifestation as we experience the most fertile months of the year and see our desires come into fruition.
- Autumn will always be there to remind us change will always arrive and that there isn't an end to anything, only a new beginning.
- We have so much to be thankful for when it comes to nature and following its seasons and cycles – because we too are nature.
- There is a perfect timing for everything in our life and nature shows us just how powerful all parts of the cycle are.
- Looking at how you can give back to Mother Earth and create more abundance only ever creates a cycle of more abundance in your life.
- If you ever want a reminder of just how beautiful, powerful, abundant and worthy you are, look at nature. It blooms in all its perfection and imperfection at just the right time and provides unlimited abundance without us even asking.
- When you tune in to nature, come home to yourself and honour your cycles, you create the space for magic and aligned abundance to flow to you.

Live with Intention

Intention, i.e. "ask", is the first step of my five-step manifestation process. The very first thing we do is set an intention when manifesting – but what does intention really mean, and how does being intentional also play into alignment and the manifesting process? Learning to be intentional has been a huge part of my alignment journey and a big breakthrough for me in terms of manifesting from an aligned space and feeling joy and alignment within myself. In this chapter, I want to help you cultivate an intentional life, learn how to be intentional with your desires and most importantly, why intentional desires attract aligned abundance.

First of all, let me take you back to Christmas 2022. I was burned out yet again and was forced to slow down after having two really bad bouts of flu and a sinus infection. My body was calling me to take it easy once again. So, I listened and during this time I felt the call to be really intentional with my desires as we headed into New Year. I've always been good at setting intentions, but I wanted to get really clear and step into this New Year with alignment, clarity and intention. I knew I wanted to up-level in big ways both in the business and in my personal life, so as I lay in bed unable to do much, I knew now was the time to get really intentional.

I used the time to purchase and complete a mini course and some webinars; these were so much fun and reminded me of how much I love to learn and throw myself into learning about spirituality for myself and not just for my work. See, I'm a pro at learning about manifesting and spirituality for my work, but I actually really enjoy learning things for myself, because eventually they feed into my work, too. This is how I realized that one of my goals for 2023 was to read more spiritual books and up-level my own practice, so that in turn I could eventually go deeper with my work, which would help me write this book.

I then found some great videos on new and exciting ways to set intentions on New Year. These included eating 12 grapes under a table at 11:59pm on New Year's Eve while thinking about 12 goals you've written down (you must finish eating the grapes by midnight) and on New Year's Day doing a cinnamon money manifesting ritual to welcome in money for the year ahead. Now, while these seemed a little extreme, I was so excited to try them and we had great fun!

The point is that what I did while ill in the run-up to New Year is because of how intentional I was with myself and my desires for that year – and how I then ended up having my most abundant year yet! Within a week of doing these things, I had my biggest financial month in the business so far and finally hit a goal within my Manifestation Membership I'd been trying to hit for years – all within a week!

Very shortly afterwards came buying our first home in February (which you read about earlier on, in chapter 8). I've already described how there was a lot stacked against us, but I knew being intentional was the key here and things were moving pretty fast. Of the extra £100,000 we needed to secure, we manifested £50,000 within a week by looking at a different lender and the other £50,000 came a week later. Talk about alignment.

Alignment had a huge part to play in buying our home, because every time I thought I'd found the perfect house, either my partner didn't like it or my parents found endless problems with it. We also didn't even know if we could borrow that much money. But I knew: "Somehow and in some way, if this house is meant to be ours it will, the money always comes and the money is always met." As I said, that mantra popped into my head very early on and I had a deep level of faith and surrender to the process. I've mentioned earlier how I said the mantra on repeat over that two-week period and each time it brought me peace and clarity. It helped me to surrender and know that if it wasn't meant to be, the Universe had another plan. Now, this level of belief in myself and the Universe has been built up over my nine years of manifesting. Once again, a reminder of the two pillars to building belief are:

1. **Lived experience:** over time as you manifest more and more things, you will start to build up a natural level of belief. This is done seamlessly as your subconscious and conscious mind have evidence that manifestation does work and there are physical examples of this in your life.
2. **Mindset:** the next pillar as you develop lived experience is to work on your mindset. You can do this by looking at your blocks, resistance, limiting beliefs or fears around receiving, worthiness and trust, for example.

Belief was one part of this manifesting story and intention was the other. I needed to have a solid level of belief in myself and the Universe to bring this into fruition, but I also needed to be incredibly intentional.

You can see from these examples just how much I was manifesting within two months of 2023 – all because of being incredibly intentional with my practice. In this time of manifesting our home I'd also manifested my highest revenue months in the business, my book *Positively Wealthy* was being sold in high-street stores nationwide and there were other incredible work opportunities. And all from sitting under the table on New Year's Eve while eating grapes, then working with cinnamon to manifest money and writing our dream-home list!

There were many little things I did over this time to be "intentional", but it was dedicating this time to my practice and my desires that allowed them to manifest so powerfully in my life. Now, there are some "lazy" ways to manifest such as subliminals (see page 28) and other manifesting exercises that you can do day to day that require next to no effort. These practices are great and I use them myself, but I believe a combination of intentional factors are required to manifest your desires effectively.

Intentional Alignment

So how does being intentional effect our alignment journey? Well, as we've seen, when we're in alignment with ourselves, we have the space and capacity to become an energetic match to our desire. Think about my example from the end of 2022: I was burned out, seeking alignment in my business, frustrated I wasn't breaking through to my next level of income and trying lots of things. The energy of this was chaotic, busy and cluttered; so how could the Universe bring in the exact things that would work for me if I was continuously busy trying lots of different stuff?

Just how often do we allow ourselves to be fully present with a task or activity? A great example of intention and alignment is when baking a cake. After all, the secret to baking the best cake is to be fully present, mindful of the recipe and to prepare to create the cake through purchasing the ingredients and carving out the time to bake it. When baking, I love being fully present – by taking in the smells, enjoying the process and seeing my creation come to life. If I breezed through this process, desperate to get to the finish line, would my cake be my best work and would I appreciate it fully once it was baked? Would it taste as good if I was distracted when baking it and rushed the process? Think about your intentions like making a cake: all the love, time and energy you put toward your cake is reflected in the end result. And approach your desires like baking a cake: would they taste as good and would you get the best result if you're not present and intentional in the process? Being intentional allows you to show up fully for your desire– and that's what your desire deserves!

Another great example is when we go all out and treat ourselves to something, whether that be an extra luxury with your weekly coffee or even buying that fancy lunchbox you saw on social media, which is going to make your daily lunch in the office extra special. Little things like this bring intention and devotion to the simplest of tasks. When we take the time to be intentional with these smaller and more insignificant activities, they spark intention in all areas of our life. I find personally that when I'm more intentional with small things like my lunch and other little activities, I'm more productive throughout my day and I find so much more joy and pleasure with my chores and tasks.

I want you to think now about the biggest desire that you'd like to call in this year. Think about how amazing it will be and how excited you are to have this in your life. Now go deeper and tune in to the energy of your desire and ask yourself: "Does my desire deserve my half-arsed energy or my fully aligned energy?"

There's your answer ... you need to show up fully to be the full expression of this desire; your desire deserves this from you and you deserve to show up fully to everything in your life. Life becomes so much more wonderful when we can become more intentional and devotional with ourselves and our desires.

A common misconception is that being intentional takes up a lot of time, when actually it doesn't; it only requires your full energy, which is the hardest part. Many struggle to find the time to be intentional, because we're always bouncing from one task to the other and one priority to another. But your desires are a priority too, and how can you expect to enjoy them once they're here if you can't be fully present with them now, in the manifesting stage? Intention is everything when it comes to manifesting: give intention to your rituals, practices and even your daily routine; they're worth your time and full energy for the result of manifesting your desire in your life. Look at this investment of your time and energy like a savings account, for example: the more intention you add to it (i.e. your life), the more benefits you'll reap as your assets grow and allow you to achieve more in your life. Starting to be intentional in your life starts with looking at the smaller tasks and activities in your life.

Romanticize your life

You might have heard of romanticizing your life before, and it's a powerful practice that I swear by. How often do we hurry through our day feeling overwhelmed and craving to be more present and joyful? Well, romanticizing your life can certainly help with this.

This doesn't have to look grand, extravagant or even Instagram-worthy – simply put, it's about what would add joy and alignment to your day. It's also a great act of self-love to find pockets of time throughout the day to be more loving with yourself, slow down and be intentional with yourself. My go-to is actually making one of my posh decaf coffees in my Nespresso machine and eating some fancy biscuits while the sun is pouring into my office. Others include taking a walk in nature on a warm sunny day and reading a good book in my garden. These are such simple things to do, yet they bring me back into my body, slow me down and reconnect me to being intentional with myself and life.

This approach is especially great if you're single and want to feel more romance in your life – it all begins with you! No matter whether you're in a relationship, married or a single Queen, you deserve your romance and to woo yourself, too.

MINIMALISM AND MANIFESTING

Minimalism works wonders with manifesting, because you create the clear space and energy for your desire to manifest. For example, once I'd shifted my mindset onto focusing on becoming the version of myself who had all of these desires and became deeply intentional instead of drifting with my desires, abundance poured in!

Being intentional doesn't mean you have to spend lots of time focusing on your desire or doing lots of complex practices. Actually, it's about the opposite! Being intentional with your manifesting helps create the space for a deeply intentional practice that actually puts energy toward your desire in an expansive way. The important part here is to show up fully. Remember the divine mirror in life: if you're not showing up fully for your desire, how can your desire show up fully in your reality?

What is Your Manifesting Superpower?

Knowing your manifesting superpower can help you to identify your strengths and also where to focus your intentional practices. The reason why so many people feel like manifesting doesn't work for them is simply because they're using the wrong tools. As I mentioned earlier, how do you know what's working or not working if you're throwing everything in the ring, so to speak? I believe there are a few different types of manifesting superpowers and establishing which one(s) you really thrive with is the key to seeing big results in your life.

As an example, it's no lie that in my work I share how much I don't connect with visualizing. I will do it, of course, if I feel called to, but the idea of sitting down and visualizing my desires each and every day sounds really boring to me. But on the flipside, I do enjoy meditating, which can be another form of visual manifesting, and I really thrive when writing and scripting (probably why I'm an author). Once I'd established that my key manifesting superpowers are writing and audio, this really helped me streamline my manifesting practices and allowed me to be more intentional with them and my desires.

I break the different types of manifesting superpowers down into the following:

Visual manifesting: if you're a visual manifestor, you love visualizing, meditating and seeing your desires come into existence. You like daydreaming and see things very clearly even before they appear in the physical. Seeing things during meditation and in your mind's eye comes very easily to you.

Audio manifesting: you love nothing more than listening as an audio manifestor! Whether that's listening to subliminals, affirmation tracks, healing frequencies, voice notes with your spiritual pals or music, anything audio-based really helps you to manifest with ease!

Vocal manifesting: if you're a vocal manifestor you love voicing your abundance! This can include voice notes to your spiritual pals, speaking your desires into existence or even recording yourself chatting as if your desire is already here. Anything where you speak into existence will be the key to attracting big abundance for you.

Written manifesting: if you're a writing manifestor then you love writing dream or goals lists, scripting, annual goals and anything that involves your hands and words! Whether that's in your lovely new journal or in the notes section on your phone, you write your dreams into reality and watch these come to life.

* * *

As I mentioned, it's perfectly normal to have one or two manifesting superpowers, and you may even dip into quite a few of these at different points in your life. However, it's not down to me to tell you what your superpower is, but instead to give you the vocabulary and awareness to highlight your unique manifesting abilities, whatever form they take. What's important to remember is that this is all about intention and by streamlining your manifesting practice to amplify your strengths in turn, you'll create joy, ease and most importantly alignment with your desire!

Bringing your big beautiful energy to your desires is only going to reflect even more big beautiful opportunities! A motto that I've always lived by along my manifesting journey is: "Big leaps bring big rewards." In order to reach our new level of abundance we must take a big leap, shed anything that's no longer serving us and align with the version of ourselves who is stepping up into this new reality. Now, it's also important to acknowledge that big leaps must feel like a hell YASS and in alignment with you, as your desires deserve your full energy and so do you!

I noticed when it previously came to major launches in my business, I'd often feel completely overwhelmed in the launch period as I'd be working on multiple projects at once. This led to me never fully being able to give my all to each launch and the results matched that "good enough but not mind-blowing" energy. It was only when I slowed down, reconnected and took on less work, that I could be fully intentional with each launch and idea. When I did this and invested all of my energy fully into each launch, each container and each idea, you can guess what happened! I in turn manifested full energy from the people in these containers. The number of comments I started to receive daily from members saying what incredible value for money and value these offerings had brought into their life blew my mind. It was like something had aligned within me and my business, which meant the results were hugely different to those before, yet all that had changed was my energy. I was bringing my big full energy to everything instead of half-assed energy and clearly this could be felt inside these offerings too. So imagine how your manifestations will feel with your full beautiful energy focused on them!

Remember, everything is energy so the more of your beautiful energy you bring to your practices and desires, the more beautiful abundantly aligned results you'll see!

What is Procrastination, Really?

Let's move deeper into what causes misalignment with intentional manifesting. On the outside, as I mentioned earlier, this can look like overwhelm, burn out and procrastination, and in some cases can even look like feeling pulled from pillar to post and not being able to give anything your full energy. If you resonate with not being able to give anything your full energy, I'd encourage you to reflect on what it is you're avoiding. What uncomfortable feelings or emotions come up when you slow down the busyness and focus on your goals? Procrastination is a form of misalignment and not prioritizing the tasks that really matter and bring you joy. So I want you to reflect on what your priorities are here in this season of your life.

Just because something doesn't feel in alignment here and now doesn't mean it won't do further down the line. The key with overwhelm and procrastination is to make sure you're prioritizing the things that really matter to you by creating the time to do them. That may look like putting a task or project on the backburner until it feels right again, to create the space for what does feel aligned for you at that moment. It could also look like scheduling block times in the morning (the first four hours are the most productive time of the day for most of us) to complete your high priority tasks so that you're not tired or stressing about it come the afternoon.

Another tip that has really helped me comes from American entrepreneur Marie Forleo's Time Genius® course, which changed my view on time forever. It's to list your current priorities, tasks and projects and rate them from 1 to 10 (with 1 being highest priority and 10 being lowest priority), based first on how much money they make you and second, how much joy they bring you. From this, I was very quickly able to prioritize the tasks that enriched my life and were important, meaning I now made time for the things that mattered.

Being Intentional Daily

Real intentional living is about focusing on the feelings during manifesting, not on control. The feelings that allow us to step up into our desired reality are created through our daily habits and our intentional practice. Remember that life is one gigantic mirror and the more intentional you are with yourself, your time and energy, the more this will be reflected back at you in all areas of life, especially in your relationships, work and manifestations. Another example might be if you were wanting to manifest love, when you'd want your partner to be deeply intentional and present with you, yes? So why aren't you being deeply intentional with yourself and your desire right now? Don't wait until it's here to start doing the intentional work; that's not how manifesting works. You must be the energetic embodiment of what you desire here and now to become the magnet that will bring it into your reality. If you want your desire to be intentional, work on intentional living in your daily life.

What stops us from being fully present are distractions that lead us away from our priorities in the moment. There are many reasons why we allow ourselves to get distracted in life and this chapter is your reminder and permission slip that beautiful things happen when we're present – and that includes aligned abundance. It could even be the past or limiting beliefs, fears or trauma that's stopping you from fully allowing yourself to be present and in the moment. What are you fearing will happen if you're present? Spend some time thinking about this and identify any potential blocks or beliefs that may be stopping you from being intentional and present in your life.

Aligned Actions

Action

A great place to start with being intentional daily is in the small mundane habits such as brushing your teeth or getting ready for the day ahead – simple tasks that most of us do on autopilot. Starting today, I want you to challenge yourself to be deeply intentional when brushing your teeth or washing the dishes, for example; pick a task and challenge yourself to be present for those two minutes of your day. Tune in to the smells, tastes, sounds around you and see what you notice as you slow down and listen. If you're doing the washing up, what do you notice as you look out of your kitchen window? What feelings arise for you as you put intention into the task at hand? You can then take your practice deeper by repeating loving affirmations in your head while brushing your teeth, for example, and use those two minutes of your morning to think positive thoughts that bring you joy and set you up for the day. Little by little, build up your intentional moments until you feel yourself noticeably becoming more present with more of your tasks and day. Eventually, you'll be living an intentional life and feel so much more fulfilment, joy and purpose – even when brushing your teeth!

Intention

I want you to think about how you can add a little self-romance to your routine. Each morning, set an intention to action this by creating the space in your day to romanticize your life with a small act or service. Think about what things you can do that would feel romantic or luxurious for you to enjoy today. Whether that's making a nice coffee for yourself at lunch or carving out the time to read a new book (it could even be this one!), decide what would feel romantic or like a treat and then action this today.

Journaling Prompts

- What does being intentional mean to me?
- What projects or tasks can I be more intentional with?
- What stops me from bringing my full energy to my desires currently?
- What am I fearing will happen if I'm present?
- How can I romanticize my day and be more intentional?
- What areas of my life do I need to romanticize more?

ALIGNED REFLECTIONS

- When we're in alignment with ourselves, we have the space and capacity to become an energetic match to our desire.
- Compare your desires to baking a cake: would the end results taste as good if you're not present and intentional in the process of creating them?
- Being intentional allows you to show up fully for your desire and that's what your desire deserves!
- Being intentional doesn't mean you have to spend lots of time focusing on your desire or doing lots of complex practices to manifest it. Actually, the opposite!
- Reflect on what your priorities are here in this season of your life.
- Intention is everything when it comes to manifesting: put intention into your rituals, practices and even daily routine. They're worth your time and full energy for the result of fulfilling your desire in your life.
- No matter whether you're in a relationship, married or a single Queen, you deserve your romance and to woo yourself too.
- Remember the divine mirror in life: if you're not showing up fully for your desire, how can your desire show up fully in your reality?
- Big leaps bring big rewards.
- Remember that everything is energy, so the more of your beautiful energy you bring to your practices and desires the more beautiful aligned abundant results you'll see!

- What uncomfortable feelings or emotions come up when you slow down the busyness and focus on your goals?
- Procrastination is about misalignment and not prioritizing the tasks that really matter and bring you joy.
- How can you know what your manifestation superpower is and what practice works if you're doing ten at once? What is your manifesting superpower?

Manifest with Joy

Magnetizing aligned abundance to yourself means getting into the vibration of joy and receiving. I love spiritual author Gabby Bernstein's description of joy being "the ultimate creator" – and it's something I live by, too, as over the years as I've seen the power of joy and how it creates the momentum for all kinds of abundance to flow into your life. If you ever want a sure way to magnetize aligned abundance to yourself quickly, get joyful and watch the magic unfold!

Now, I know that's easier said than done when we live in a world full of challenges and complexities that, of course, zap our joy. It's also not sustainable to be high-vibe and joyful all of the time. The Law of Polarity states that everything has an opposite, and the existence of these opposites is vital in helping us to gain a deeper perspective of our own lives and necessary for balance within our Universe. This energetic law teaches us that we need these down and sad days to be able to understand and appreciate joyful and happy days. This is the Law of Polarity at its core: that duality exists in everything. Neither could exist without its opposite. So it's not about suppressing the bad days or trying to force your way into a positive vibration; it's all about flowing and allowing yourself to align with the energy you're in.

So why joyful manifesting? Over my years of awareness around the Law of Attraction, I've tried and tested many ways to manifest, as you can imagine. Through my own experiences, my communities and while writing my books, I've experimented with what really streamlines the manifestation process and supercharges attracting your desires to you. What I've discovered is that joy sits at the heart of the vibration we need to emanate to manifest more uplifting experiences into our life and our manifestations as a whole.

Of course, there are many fun ways to cultivate more joy in your life and it definitely starts with the small day-to-day things that spark joy, as these add up to the bigger moments in life and your manifestations. In this chapter, I'm going to share some ideas to get you started. The more joy you experience day to day, the more fulfilled, happy and positive you'll feel, which will make you an incredible magnet to aligned abundance!

Create the Space for Joy

First of all, we've got to create the space for joy. As with any manifestation, we need to let go of the old to be able to welcome in the new by creating the space for it. As you'll have learned in chapter 5, we must create the space physically, emotionally and spiritually to up-level and welcome in the energy of aligned abundance. The same goes for joy: we must identify what zaps us of joy and clear and remove this as necessary.

I was actually reminded of this only this week, when I was hosting my annual "5 Days to Alignment and Joy Challenge" with over 2,000 of you, which reminded me of my own expectations around the people in my life and how this had really been zapping my joy recently. As if by magic, when I released these expectations, raised my vibration and aligned with joy again, I felt true joy again! So look at your expectations in all areas of your life – of your loved ones, in work, at home, of yourself and your desires. Make a commitment to release these expectations today and see how much lighter you feel from just doing this!

Maybe it's something physical zapping joy from your life; for example, maybe it's a job you know is no longer aligned for you, maybe you've been reaching for the wine on a Saturday night a little too often and this has been killing your vibe, or you've neglected your yoga or fitness routine for a while and keep telling yourself you'll get back on it! We all know how we sabotage our joy by not prioritizing the things that really matter to us and bring us happiness. Even if it's challenging yourself to go to sleep 30 minutes earlier tonight so you feel more rested, set yourself up for success and make a commitment to prioritize the things that spark joy in your life.

Looking at joy on a deeper level, recreation and pursuing our passions make us so much happier, creative, productive and peaceful. Many people rush from place to place to keep up with their professional obligations, social commitments and endless to-do lists, while ignoring the needs of their soul in the process. They may find that the weeks will slip into months and months into years, and the years into decades, without ever truly experiencing joy. Now, that's not the life you came here to lead, is it, Queen?

Raise Your Vibration

The fastest way to tap back into joy is by raising your vibration (your energy or frequency that you're vibrating at). This is one of my favourite things to do to feel aligned with myself again. The key to raising your vibration is to move your body, moving stuck or stagnant energy through you to ground back in and regulate yourself. The reason why our vibration lowers is because of lower frequency emotions like sadness, for example, as this becomes stuck and stagnant in our energy, body and mind. You'll notice how if you're having a bad day and you lie down or sit around, you feel no better when you eventually do get up. Yet when we go outside for a walk or exercise, we'll feel a world of difference as we've moved those lower frequency emotions and feelings through our body. For more ideas on how to raise your vibration, turn back to chapter 2, but most of all make sure that you have fun!

Flow

Flowing with the Universe requires divine surrender, trust and getting into a state of flow. Similar to how the mindset of "going with the flow" requires a degree of releasing control, not force, flow in its literal sense means experiencing flow in a project or task, when you may be so focused that you immerse yourself for hours and hours in it. In the manifestation sense, a state of flow means being in the stream of abundance and feeling aligned with flow in all of its forms. Aligned abundance will flow to you through surrendered manifesting and trust (see chapter 14).

Become Magnetic

As I've witnessed my life unfold during my manifestation journey, I've leaned more and more into magnetic practices and learning how to relax into being a manifestation magnet. Just like actual magnets, a manifestation magnet doesn't repel, it attracts; as the famous saying goes, "I don't chase, I attract." Be a magnet and allow abundance to be attracted to you. Getting into flow state and raising your vibration will both help you to become that vibrant magnet.

Now, this entire book is about helping you become magnetic to your desires and abundance, but I want you to look at your mindset around being a magnet to positivity, abundance and all good things. Do you believe you are a magnet to these things currently? The real secret to becoming magnetic is knowing that your desire is already yours and that it gets to be fun! How much more magnetic do you feel right now, just by knowing that your desire is already yours?

Joy is the ultimate creator, so by embodying joy you become a magnet to many wonderful things and you get to have fun in the process. A great affirmation I love to work with is this:

"Universe, show me how good it gets to be. Manifesting my desires gets to be fun, and joyful."

Repeat this today and see how much fun you can have throughout your day! Remember, too, that what is meant to be yours is already yours.

Connect with Your Core Energy of Desire

Connecting to the true essence of our being and desires connects us back to our truth and removes the blocks and limitations that we place on ourselves and our desires. The reason why this practice alone will bring you huge shifts and results is because it takes you straight to the core energy of your desire and you get to spend intentional time with this. This means you get to spend quality time with your desire BEFORE it's even manifested into your reality, which is magnetic in itself. Spending time with your desire allows you to magnetize it into your energy field and reality, while also grounding you back into its true essence, free from your expectations and human limitations.

I first channelled this practice five years ago and adore it so much that I dedicated a whole chapter to this method in my book *Hurt, Healing, Healed*. I used it to manifest my now fiancé; I spent time with this energy often, knowing it was my dream relationship, and when we met a few months later and our relationship gently got underway, I knew this was my manifestation, as I recognized his energy instantly. Using this joyful manifesting method will also allow you to identify if something is your manifestation and it's a great surrender practice if you feel attached or controlling of your desire. By working with the core energy of your desire, you'll get straight to the end goal and quickly!

If you'd like to try this powerful meditation for yourself, you can find it in the resources page for this book at: www.emmamumford.co.uk/alignedabundance. I would recommend doing this meditation often to get familiar with the core energy of your desire and to magnetize this to you. Feel how magnetic your desire feels after doing this meditation and releasing any limitations or expectations around it.

Co-create with the Universe

Remember that manifestation is a co-creation experience: you go halfway and the Universe meets you halfway too. The biggest zappers of joy are control, expectations and attachment. If you've tried the Aligned Actions in chapter 6, you'll likely be feeling more joy naturally as you've continued to journey through the book and the exercises. Joyful manifesting comes from a place of surrender, nonattachment and openness with your intentions. When I'm joyfully manifesting, I stay open to the Universe surprising me with the sort of desires and abundance I wasn't even focusing on or looking for. This is the power of joy: you become the ultimate magnet to all of the aligned abundance available to you.

Remember that Old Ways won't Open New Doors

When hitting the reset button and tapping back into joyful manifesting, remember that old ways won't open new doors. If you've been attempting to climb out of a manifesting or joy rut but to no avail, then trying something new to shift the energy will create a different result. Aligning with your desired reality requires you to try new things, shake up the energy and up-level into the version of yourself who has your desire. This is why

I regularly make myself experiment with new things and new manifesting techniques, so I can expand and challenge myself to open new doors and see what these experiences bring.

If your manifesting practice has started to feel stuck or stagnant, for example, and it's not bringing you the joy or high vibes it used to, then this is a sure sign to try something new! Mix it up and try another door. We can't keep trying the same door, getting stuck and then expecting the result to be different the next time we do exactly the same thing. It's time to up-level your approach through the suggestions in this chapter to magnetize the new reality that you desire.

Use Expanders

Expanders have been one of the most joyful ways I've been able to tap into new levels of abundance and joy in my life over the last few years. For example, many people have asked me on podcast interviews whether my previous couponing business and money-saving mindset has changed or shifted since becoming a manifestation teacher. Now, of course I ran my couponing business over 10 years ago, so I've naturally up-levelled and shifted how I see things as I've entered my thirties and understand energy and manifestation more. However, I do still stand by the fact that couponing in particular can help us to align with new financial levels we may not be able to tap into quite yet.

I use couponing as an abundance expander to experience the things I want now, not when I have the money. For example, if owning that new Dyson hairdryer would help you align with the version of yourself who has fulfilled your money desire and to expand into the frequency of feeling abundant and wealthy, then why wouldn't you use a discount code to make that your reality now? How much better does it feel having that item *and* it feeling in alignment?

I've heard many people say to me over the years, "But Emma, that's all very well and good, but I can't quite stretch to purchasing that right now – even though it would get me closer to my desire." I hear you and I feel you, and no, putting your purchase on a credit card probably wouldn't feel aligned and may even cause you more anxiety, which is not the vibration of joyful manifesting! However, if you can get a 20 per cent-off voucher, which makes that purchase then feel like a hell YASS to you, then why wouldn't you use a coupon as an expander to get you into the reality you desire to experience? These sorts of expanders show you what's possible in a way that's attainable for your current level of finances and mindset.

Now a coupon won't work for every scenario in life, of course, but if that new laptop would help you to up-level your business and manifest the goals you've set, then do use expanders like coupons and discounts to help you get to where you want to be in a way that feels aligned here and now. Another example of an expander could look like booking a discounted night away at a dream luxury hotel to help you get into the energy and vibration of that lifestyle here and now. Although I went from Coupon Queen to Spiritual Queen over nine years ago, you can still catch me using coupons, cash back and discounts to expand myself into new levels of abundance. I personally don't feel it limits me, as I've been able to attract and achieve every income level that I've set out for myself so far. It's what works for you at the end of the day and what brings you closer to joy. And don't forget that coupons, cash back and discounts count as money manifestations too, as that's money staying in your bank!

Connect with Your Joyful Inner Child

Finally, one of my favourite ways to manifest joy is with your inner child! Our inner child is part of our psyche that we carry with us throughout our life. Remember that magic you used to feel as a child? Where anything was possible and unicorns and fairies existed at the bottom of the garden? That magic never disappeared; we just grew up. Life starts to zap that joy as we become adults and disconnect us from the inner child within us who wants to play and experience joy. Working with your inner child allows you to tap back into that joy and unlock a whole new level of joy and abundance in your adult life. Prioritize the joy you and your inner child want to unlock in your life and watch the abundant magic start to unfold.

Now, if you've never done inner child work before then don't worry, the meditation at the end of this chapter (located in the book's resources) will help you connect with yours and guide you on how to work with them. While many people will know about inner child work through their healing journey, not everyone knows you can also manifest with your inner child and how they're the secret to unlocking more joy and alignment in your life. Hence why I created an entire course I've run for the last six years called "Inner Child Joy". When we align within ourselves first of all in the aligned abundance process, we're also aligning with our inner child, as they are part of us that wants to be expressed too. I also believe that the inner critic/ego is our inner child, so instead of having a go at your inner critic the next time it pipes up, speak to it gently and show it love (it's part of you after all). If you do this consistently, you'll notice the negative inner chatter and comments will also quieten down as your inner child begins to feel seen and heard.

Build a Joyful Mindset

The above practices and tools will help you manifest amazing things joyfully into your life and will positively impact your beliefs and mindset over time. Building a joyful mindset through consistent actions will also help you to tap into joy more frequently and navigate challenging times too. Just like everything in this chapter, building a joyful mindset gets to be easy and it gets to be fun!

To make a start, look at the Aligned Actions below and challenge yourself to do one small thing each day to spark joy in your life. You see, those small seemingly insignificant moments really do add up. Commit to a playful approach to manifesting your desires – get curious and experiment, because it would be really fun to experience that desire, involve your inner child and most importantly have fun. Life is too short not to be in the magnetic energy of living your life and joy!

Aligned Actions

Action

Every day, for the next 21 days, challenge yourself to do one small thing to spark joy in your day. It may be something I've suggested to raise your vibration, or it could be something else your inner child wants to do just for fun. Find a small window of time and commit to doing one joyful thing. It could take you 10 seconds or 10 minutes – it doesn't matter as long as you experience joy. You might find it helpful to plan ahead what you'll do for joy the next day, or even the whole week ahead. Set yourself up for success and create the time in your day to commit to joy. Doing this practice for 21 days straight will help you to cultivate more joyful moments in your life and, just like practising gratitude, will help you to see how much joy you can find around you, especially in those small and seemingly mundane moments.

Intention

Head to the resources for this book at www.emmamumford. co.uk/alignedabundance to access my "Joyful Manifesting" meditation, designed to help you tap into inner child joy and embody the magnetic energy in this chapter. Journal about what your inner child shares with you and anything else that comes through in the meditation. Make sure to action these responses where possible.

Journaling Prompts

- When did I last feel magnetic to abundance?
- What was I doing at that point in time?
- What am I ready to let go of to welcome in expansion and this new up-levelled energy in my life?
- What expanders can I work with to invite in joyful manifesting?
- How can I spark more joy in my life?
- What manifesting practices feel good and spark joy for me?
- When do I feel most joyful?
- What does my inner child want to do for fun this week?

ALIGNED REFLECTIONS

- If you ever want a sure way to magnetize aligned abundance to you quickly, get joyful and watch the magic unfold!
- It's not about suppressing the bad days or trying to force your way into a positive vibration; it's about flowing and allowing yourself to align with the energy you're in.
- The more joy you experience day to day, the more fulfilled, happy and positive you'll feel, which will make you an incredible magnet to the most aligned abundance!

- Set yourself up for success and make a commitment to prioritize the things that spark joy in your life.
- The real secret to becoming magnetic is knowing that your desire is already yours and that it gets to be fun! How much more magnetic do you feel right now just by knowing that your desire is already yours?
- A great affirmation I love to work with is: "Universe, show me how good it gets to be. Manifesting my desires gets to be fun, and joyful." Repeat this today and see how much fun you can have throughout your day!
- Connecting to the true essence of our being and desires connects us back to our truth and removes the blocks and limitations that we place on ourselves and our desires.
- Joyful manifesting comes from a place of surrender, nonattachment and openness with your intentions.
- Building a joy mindset through consistent actions will also help you to tap into joy more frequently and navigate challenging times, too.
- Those small, seemingly insignificant moments really do add up to the big moments of joy in our life.
- Commit to a playful approach to manifesting your desires: get curious and experiment, involve your inner child and most importantly have fun. Life is too short not to be in the magnetic energy of living your life and joy!
- Working with your inner child allows you to unlock a whole new level of joy and abundance in your adult life. Prioritize the joy you and your inner child want to unlock in your life and watch the abundant magic start to unfold.

Embody the Abundant Version of Yourself

Embodiment practices are one of my absolute favourite manifestation tools; firstly, they're so much fun to work with and secondly, you can magnetize abundance to yourself incredibly quickly when you change the way you see manifestation and what the process really is. In chapter 1, we looked briefly at the importance of embodiment when it comes to manifesting aligned abundance. This chapter is going to change how you view manifesting forever …

I'd like you to approach this chapter almost like a hack to manifestation. Now, don't get me wrong – I'm a Virgo and I LOVE a process! Hence why I've been sharing my five-step manifesting process since 2018, which has helped thousands of people like yourself change the way they see manifestation and finally have practical and tangible steps that make sense and break the process down. But in life we'd all love a cheat sheet or hack to get everything we want here and now. In my book *Hurt, Healing, Healed*, I shared that sadly there are no quick fixes to attract your goal, which remains true. However, I've since discovered that alignment practices can supercharge our energy and desires, essentially bringing them to us effortlessly and without drawn-out practices. Which is a big hell YASS from me!

Over the years, I've devoted myself to so many lengthy manifestation processes and of course some worked, but most didn't. I believe they didn't work because I wasn't aware of my manifesting superpowers and honouring the practices, tools and modalities that really resonated with me, and also because I became addicted to the inner work and hustling for my desires too. It's funny, but only the other day I was looking at some old footage on my Manifestation Membership platform when I noticed an old print I had above my desk that said "Success comes to those who work their ass off." That quote began to feel out of alignment for me, so I replaced it with a calm beach image, which felt way more relaxing when I was working. But seeing this quote again after all these years reminded me of how much my own mindset has shifted around work and, of course, my manifestations.

Less is More

You see, in the old-school teachings of manifestation that we know and love, we're taught that we must give 110 per cent to see results; that we must do all the exercises and tools daily to make our success inevitable. I now believe this was sign of the times, as since the lockdowns in 2020 we're doing less now as a collective and wanting a more healthy relationship with receiving from the Universe without feeling constantly overwhelmed and overstimulated. The number one reason why I see people fall off the manifesting bandwagon is because it isn't sustainable for them; it might work for a week or two but very quickly life happens and they stop their daily practices and feel full of shame and fear that they've missed a day. Well, the Universe won't punish you for missing a day – it's not a presence that punishes people at all. It's an energy that is responding to you and, yes, it's okay to take a day off and to honour your alignment and flow.

In my own healing around the divine feminine energy and workaholism, I unpacked so much around why I controlled my manifestations, went 90 per cent of the way to meet the Universe instead of 50, and why I kept reading all the books, doing all the practices and more – only to see inconsistent results. Yet when I did less, guess what? More starting flowing. I was working with a very important mantra at the time, which was "Emma does less, Emma attracts more". So of course this would be helping the process and was quite literally manifesting into my life. But if we take it back to chapter 5 on decluttering, then we know that actually by doing less we create the space for more in our life and the space for new energy and abundance to flow our way.

The Greatest Manifestation Secret

So why is this chapter the greatest manifestation hack? It's because it's actually not about cheating the process at all; it's more about streamlining things to the benefit of your aligned abundance. You see, everything is energy. However, we often get so focused on the human process that we forget we're dealing with mind, body and spirit to manifest our desires. So in this chapter, we're going to be working with the spiritual side of manifesting (the quantum realm) and energy. Many overlook the energetic realm when manifesting, but we manifest through energy, we are energy and everything is energy – and so we can create energy in manifestation and skip the unnecessary practices that don't bring us any closer to alignment or our desire.

The practices that don't get you closer to your desires are keeping you stuck in this current reality and version of your life. You see, to manifest your desired outcome you must *become* the version of yourself who has this desire (also known as the "acting as if" practice). Now, to become this version of yourself, yes, some inner work may be required to remove any blocks or beliefs that stop you from being this person currently, but the good news is you already are the version of you who has ALL of your heart's desires. You don't need a whole personality transplant – phew! You are already the very you who will receive a lifetime of aligned abundance.

Let's go back to our radio analogy from earlier in the book: you don't buy a whole new radio to switch stations; you simply tune the frequency to what you desire and – BOOM – the very song you know all the words to comes on and your energy changes immediately as you sing away and enjoy the song! This is what happens when you align with your highest timeline and aligned abundance: the song feels sooo good and you feel like an entirely different person, even though you're still you! So in this chapter, we're going to be focusing on tuning into your highest timeline and changing the frequency in your life to attract huge abundance without all the long drawn-out processes. Now, of course, there are still steps to this but they're lots of fun and don't involve arm ache from writing your desire down 55 times for five days (yes, I did this old school method once and never again!).

First, let's remind ourselves of the two pillars of alignment:

1st Pillar – alignment within yourself: Coming into alignment with abundance requires you to come into alignment within yourself first. This can look like aligning within your mind, body and spirit; reconnecting; grounding back in; discovering and expressing your authentic self; strengthening your intuition; honouring your body; making aligned decisions and knowing when to walk away from what's no longer serving you and keeping you stuck.

2nd Pillar – alignment with your desire: Once you're experiencing alignment internally, this can now be reflected into the outer world through flow, abundance and aligning on a vibrational level with the version of yourself who has your desire. This can look like flowing over forcing; embodying the emotions and feelings of your desired outcome; becoming the version of you who has your desire through embodiment practices; magnetizing your new reality to you; taking aligned and inspired action to meet the Universe halfway and surrendering to the divine plan for your life.

* * *

Now, let's first dive into the first pillar more closely as we start to explore the embodiment side of manifesting.

Aligned Decisions

As we saw in chapter 1, making empowered choices and decisions in your life is a key step in the alignment process. When you feel uncertain about what to do, remember to ask yourself:

> Is this bringing me closer to my desired outcome or further away?

As an example, if a work opportunity came up, yet I also had book deadlines that were my aligned priority, I would ask myself whether the work opportunity would bring me closer to my desire of writing the most incredible book or take me further away from it.

You will have to tune in to your own intuition to answer this question for yourself, as there will be all kinds of decisions to make in life where you'll need to use your discernment – and that is what alignment is all about! We don't have a crystal ball that will tell us whether our decisions will be a lesson or a blessing, but we do have our internal compass, our intuition.

Our intuition, also known as our gut instinct, third eye chakra and connection to Source, is the innate wisdom within us all that allows us to connect to our truth. Your intuition will never let you down, although your ego can step in and confuse you – and this is why many doubt their intuition. If you can't trust yourself, how can you expect yourself to trust the Universe? The inner always reflects the outer, so as we explored in chapter 8, "Trust the Universe", trust is built within trusting yourself and your body first.

Your intuition is like a muscle that must be built over time. You wouldn't expect to walk into a gym on your first day and have impressive abs and quads. It takes time, it takes consistency and it takes nurturing. Think about it: if you were to listen deeply to someone and trust them, they would want to open up to you more and share with you more frequently. So trust those niggles, trust those sensations in your body and trust the words or feelings that arise as you make a decision.

I've always known within myself if it's not a "hell, YASS" it's a "hell, no". When exciting new opportunities come in, I usually get a sense there and then whether I feel drawn to exploring them. I feel open, flowing, excited, certain and expansive; whereas any opportunities that make me feel anxious, indecisive, stuck in decision mode, restricting and would mean compromise I know are a divine "hell no". Not that I always listen to that response the first time round and of course we do have to make some compromises in life; that's the Law of Polarity once again at play. Usually, I know whether it's an aligned compromise that doesn't take anything away from me or whether it's a question of people pleasing and I'm sacrificing my joy or alignment to make something happen.

Knowing the difference between your ego and intuition is important when leaning into your intuition and strengthening this. Here is how I define the two and what I look out for when making decisions:

- **Intuition:** calm; all one pitch; certain; short, profound words; will be the same answer if you ask again; calms the nervous system; expansive; feels loving and safe even if it's not the answer you wanted.

- **Ego:** dramatic; tempo will change; normally negative; long, drawn-out messages; will not feel right; will change each time it answers; will feel fearful; constrictive; stressful to your nervous system.

Everyone is different, and you'll start to identify your key ego versus your intuition indicators as you feel into your body, nervous system and soul. You might feel a sensation in your stomach that feels constricting, for example, or you might feel light and joyful. Get to know your body and the signs it gives you as you learn to slow down and listen to your inner compass.

If you're following your intuition and inner truth, your inner compass will never steer you wrong. It can feel scary to say no to seemingly positive opportunities and abundance that flows your way. However, as we know, saying no to what takes you further away from fulfilling your desire then creates the space for you to align even quicker with the aligned opportunities that bring you closer to aligned abundance. I've definitely felt scared over the years saying no, but the peace I feel when I do say no to things that don't align with me helps to bring me an abundance of the most incredible manifestations shortly after.

Align with Your Desire

So far, I've mainly been walking you through the first pillar of alignment and focusing on aligning with yourself first in this book. Now, I want to turn our focus going forward on aligning with your desire. I want to start off with a fun exercise that will get you thinking about your optimal timeframe and where some energetic alignment may still need to be done.

I want you to focus on the one desire you really want to manifest as a result of reading this book so far. Grab your journal and pen and pick the first desire that comes into your mind and write down your answers to the prompts below. (If you'd like to tune in and get into the flow with this exercise, you can find my "Embodying the Abundant Version of Yourself" visualization for these prompts in the resources this book at: www.emmamumford.co.uk/alignedabundance)

Embodying the Abundant Version of Yourself
Journal Prompts

- What does this version of myself who has my desire do each day?
- What are they wearing?
- How are they feeling?
- Who are they with?
- What is something they do each day that I don't do currently?
- What is this version of myself who has my desire worried about?

If you've done the visualization mentioned above, don't forget to write down the wisdom shared with you from your higher self so you can action this.

Embody Your Desired Self's Feelings and Emotions

Were there any key emotions or feelings that came up in the visualization or when answering the prompts above? Now that you've gained deeper insight into this aligned and abundant version of yourself, you need to work on embodying the feelings and emotions that this version of yourself experiences.

I want you to get into the mode of what a millionaire (if that's your desire, for example) or a person with your dream job would do on a daily basis. Think about how a millionaire would brush their teeth, get dressed in the morning, drive to work, eat lunch, work out at the gym, interact with their loved ones, eat dinner, prepare for bed and go to sleep. Go through an entire day of the life you desire and write down exactly how the abundant version of yourself would brush your teeth, work out, eat your meals and even rest. You may think this sounds bizarre but, believe me, when we can identify the habits of your desired reality, then you can start to embody these here and now, which will magnetize the same frequency and, in turn, manifest your desire.

Now, when you write your "day in the life" list (see page 183 for the Aligned Action), you may realize that the version of yourself who's working at your dream role can't just turn up at a new place of work and waltz in, pretending you already work there. We don't want to have you escorted off the premises! But in your spare time, you could still drive the route you would take to your dream job and experience what it feels like to travel to that new place of work. You could visit the showroom for your dream car and test drive it; you could view the houses you desire as if you are ready to purchase and move in. These are all aligned actions.

Even if you can't physically go out and experience your desire right away, you can absolutely start with the micro habits of your abundant self's daily routine. For example, you can begin to embody brushing your teeth like a millionaire by upgrading your toothbrush if that feels aligned and matches the vision you have of this abundant version of yourself. I did this recently after my dentist had encouraged me to upgrade my electric toothbrush. It was luckily around Black Friday too, which meant I got a very nice upgrade for a fraction of the price. Now whenever I brush my teeth they feel so much cleaner, my brushing has improved with the assisted app and I feel more luxurious, knowing I'm looking after my teeth in an aligned way. So write your "day in the life" list and start to action these micro habits, whether it's with an intentional lunch, an expansive afternoon or upgrading a piece of furniture in your home. Start stepping into this abundant version of yourself now by aligning your micro habits with your desired daily life.

An example of the power of this approach comes from the lovely Jessica. We'd been working together for a few months, during which time she'd been hoping to land her dream acting role. We'd gone through any resistance she might have to attracting this job and now it was time for the embodiment part. I walked Jessica through the above journaling prompts and she said that the abundant version of herself who had her dream role would sit on the balcony of her London flat each morning in a nice floral dress and drink coffee. So I said, "Great, do exactly that for the next week and let me know how you get on!" Five days later, Jessica emailed me to let me know her dream acting role had manifested with ease!

This is a great example to share here, as so many people get caught up in the "how" they are going to manifest something. Instead, Jessica's coffee example had nothing to do with the acting role really, but in her mind that was the representation of her manifestation and what her aligned abundance looked and felt like. Through embodying this over the five days, she then stepped into her highest timeline and manifested her dream role.

Dive Deeper into Embodiment

So what exactly is embodiment and how can we align with this in the manifesting process? By definition, embodiment means "tangible or visible form of an idea, quality, or feeling", meaning in this context that you experience the desired reality in mind, body and spirit. You are an embodiment of the very feelings and emotions you wish to experience in the physical. To me personally, embodiment means walking my talk, bringing my manifestation into the body through energy work and my energetic field; it means feeling, seeing, hearing and experiencing my desire through mind, body and spirit. Alignment is very much a mind, body and spirit experience, so we must focus on all three when moving through this process.

Another factor to consider in the embodiment journey is that time is an illusion. Yes, in human form we do experience time, but time doesn't actually exist in the Universe itself. Only alignment does. So if you're not experiencing your desire in the physical world just yet, this is because of alignment rather than the result of so-called "divine timing". As we saw earlier, many people get hung up on time and sit around patiently waiting for a green light from the Universe, which is how you then get stuck in cycles and patterns, and can end up looking back and realizing you've been in the same place for months or even years! When you eliminate time from the manifestation process, you align with the knowing that all that stands in between you and your desire is alignment and what you are in line with.

Alignment, to me, means what you are in line with in terms of your energy and vibration. During my alignment journey over the last few years, I soon noticed that my manifestations and abundance came to me more quickly than expected. I tapped into the state of flow more easily and aligned abundance surprises would come in regularly, exceeding any expectations that I had. One of those reasons was what I like to call "hacking the process". Now don't get me wrong, we can't bypass anything in life or in the manifestation process. What we resist persists. So I'm not suggesting you avoid or bypass anything along your journey; the opposite actually, as the quickest way to the end is through! But we can speed up this process through alignment and that's where it feels like you're hacking the process, when actually you're just getting straight to the core and magnetizing this to you.

Stop Asking Again for your Desire

So often I see people get stuck in the asking step of manifesting by repeating affirmations, scripting, setting the same intention, visualizing it and sometimes doing all of these things daily! When we overwhelm ourselves, we create restriction, and our energy and space become cluttered with practices, instead of full of the energy needed to manifest. So if you feel overwhelmed by your daily practice and can identify with continually asking, this is why you're feeling stuck.

You only need ask once: the Universe has your order and is already getting to work. Imagine yourself in a cafe with a friend. Your friend has placed their order and you place yours with the waitress. But then you keep repeating your order for a decaf coffee. After a moment, the waitress would get pretty annoyed that you're keeping her there when she knows your order and wants to start making it, but can't as you keep asking her for the same drink over and over again. The Universe knows what coffee or desire you want to fulfil, as you've already placed your order the first time of asking.

Another way I see people getting caught up in the process is by obsessing over practices. Very often in my weekly Instagram Q&As, I'll get asked questions about doing more; for example, "Should I be doing more practices?" Or, "What practices work and how many practices should I be doing daily?" Great questions, but there's following an alignment process and then there's obsessing over a process that keeps you stuck. Don't get caught up in the process when you want the end result!

If you're someone who obsesses over doing things "right", a great way to resolve this is by focusing on the end result and actually working backward. Instead of focusing on the process and where you're now in it, think about how your life will be when your desire is here. What habits will you be doing daily when it's here? Remember those questions I asked you earlier on in this chapter with the visualization – it's exactly that! It's about identifying the end result and working backward from there. So if that version of yourself feels happy and joyful, what steps can you take over the next three months to embody those emotions here and now? If that version of yourself wears a lovely red dress to their dream job, then how can you start wearing that red dress now?

By working backward, you embody these aligned feelings and emotions here and now; and you stop focusing on practices that keep you stuck in the current version of yourself. When you focus on working backward through your desired emotions and feelings, you align with your highest timeline and you allow whatever practices or tools that may need to be done to fall into your path as they're meant to. Manifesting isn't about how many practices you can do or about any practices at all, really – it all comes down to your energy, beliefs and identities and what reality you're aligning with. Practices simply help us to achieve the desired energy needed in the manifestation process, but the amount you do doesn't determine the inevitability of fulfilling your desires.

This exercise is especially great if you're someone who struggles to see the whole staircase when taking action toward your desires. You don't need to see or know the whole staircase; you only need take your next best step. What is your next best step toward embodying your desire? What action can you start to take this week?

Remember, nothing is ever right or wrong as long as it feels right to you. The Universe will not punish you or anyone for listening to themselves and adapting practices to feel good to you, so trust your intuition.

Know that Your Desire is Manifesting You, Too

So often we can get caught up in thinking it's only us who wants that dream house, job, partner or holiday, when it works both ways. Something I really want you to embody more than anything in this chapter is that your desire wants you too!

A great example of this was when I was manifesting the home we now live in. I got so caught up in the human blocks of money and the "hows" that I forget the house wanted us too! It wasn't just about me manifesting this house, our house was manifesting us living there as well. I shared this reminder in my recent Manifesting Challenge, and set the task for everyone to write down why their manifestation wanted them. That day, we had so many incredible shifts in the group and some people even saw their desires manifest after months of feeling blocked!

At the end of this chapter, you will find an exercise that you can do for one desire or a couple of them. Don't underestimate the power of this embodying exercise, as when we ground back into the knowing that our desire wants us and is seeking us too, we remember that we're not doing this alone. What you're seeking is seeking you too. You want it so badly because you already have it in the future.

I want you to read that again. Embodying the abundant version of yourself means knowing that your desire is already yours and that you're feeling all this attachment, frustration and want right now, because at some level you know you're actually experiencing your desire in the future. What a plot twist that is for the part of you that might not believe it can happen yet!

Embody Your Feelings

I want to shift focus slightly onto feelings and emotions as we wrap up one of the most important chapters in this book, and why these are some of the most important energies you can embody in the manifesting process. To me, embodiment is a mind, body, spirit experience, as we weave the energetics of our desire into our energy field (spirit), mind (cognitive) and body (physical). Manifestation uses all three and it's through the process of embodiment that we bring our desires into actualization. The quickest way to embodiment is through feelings and emotions and bringing these frequencies into the here and now.

In fact, the true essence of manifestation is feeling and emotion, and having witnessed so many examples of this, I do believe that their energy trumps all. Yes, our words and thoughts do create our reality, but I believe it's our consistent energy and vibration that magnetize our reality to us. When it comes to your desire, it's not the manifestation as such that you want; it's a feeling or experience – so tap into whichever feeling or emotional experience your desire is rooted in and start to embody those feelings from today. If your feeling is joy, for example, start by cultivating more joy in your life through your daily habits and aligned decisions.

Remember, you attract what you are; not what you want. So who are you right now? Are you the abundant version of yourself who has your desire?

I'm so excited to see the shifts and breakthroughs you experience as a result of this chapter. This is my absolute favourite work to do and implementing these new habits, feelings and emotions is the quickest way to reach your aligned abundance!

Aligned Actions

Action

Write down why your desire wants you. Go deep with this, you can do this just for one desire or with a couple of them. Here's an example of what I wrote down about our house, along with some extra examples:

- My dream house wants me because I'm great at interior design and can't wait to turn our house into a loving home.
- My dream home wants me because it wants to grow and expand with our energy.
- My dream career wants me because I'm incredibly organized and do a great job.
- My dream partner wants me because I'm kind, caring and love making people laugh.

You could even write your own versions on a sticky note and put this somewhere you'll see it often to remind you of why your desire wants you too!

As an extra bonus intentional task, I want you to write down "a day in the life" list, describing the version of yourself who has your desire already. (You can use your answers from the "Embodying the Abundant Version of Yourself" exercise on page 179 in this chapter.) Write down everything this version of yourself does – from the moment they wake up until they go to sleep, including their habits and meals. Get descriptive and really tap into what this version of yourself is feeling and doing daily.

You could write it out in a scripting/journaling format or like a schedule, whatever feels most aligned for you. For example:

7:30am – I wake up feeling positive and refreshed after a great night's sleep. I then pick up my journal and start my expansive daily practice for the day that feels so good.

Once you've finished your "a day in the life" list, it's time to start working backward and implementing this now! It may help to write down some actions you can take in the coming week, month and three months to embody this.

Intention

Grab your journal and pen, and focus on the one desire you really want to manifest as a result of reading this book. Pick the first one that comes into your mind and write down your answers to the prompts below. If you'd like to get into the flow with this exercise, you can find my "Embodying The Abundant Version Of Yourself" visualization for these prompts in the book's resources available at www.emmamumford.co.uk/alignedabundance. If you've done this visualization, don't forget to write down the wisdom shared with you from your higher self so you can action this.

Journal Prompts

- What does the version of myself who has my desire do each day?
- What are they wearing?
- How are they feeling?
- Who are they with?
- What do they do each day that I don't do currently?
- What is the version of myself who has my desire worried about?
- What action can I take to step into this abundant version of myself?
- What has been my biggest takeaway from this chapter?

ALIGNED REFLECTIONS

- The Universe won't punish you for missing a day; it's not a presence that punishes people at all. It's an energy that's responding to you and, yes, it's okay to take a day off and honour your alignment and flow.
- The good news is you already are the version of you who has ALL of your heart's desires. You don't need a whole personality transplant – phew! You are already the very you who will receive a lifetime of aligned abundance.
- When feeling uncertain about a decision, ask yourself, "Is this bringing me closer to my desired outcome or further away?"

- We don't have a crystal ball that will tell us whether our decisions will be a lesson or a blessing, but what we do have is our internal compass, our intuition.
- Get to know your body and the signs it gives you as you learn to slow down and listen to your inner compass.
- Saying no to what takes you further away from your desire creates the space for you to align even more quickly with the aligned opportunities that bring you closer to aligned abundance.
- When we can identify the micro habits in the desired reality, we can embody these here and now to magnetize the same frequency, which in turn will manifest our desire.
- When you focus on working backward with your desired emotions and feelings, you align with your highest timeline and allow whatever practices or tools that may need to be done to fall into your path as they're meant to.
- What you're seeking is seeking you too.
- When it comes to your desire it's not the manifestation as such you want, it's a feeling or experience; so tap into whatever feeling, emotion or experience your desire is rooted in and start to embody those feelings from today.

PART TWO

Flow with Alignment

"Life is like a river. The way of life is to flow with the current. To turn against it takes effort but the current will carry you if you let it. Float with joy and ease."

Anonymous

Now that you've embarked on a deeply transformational alignment journey in Part One and uncovered your alignment blocks, it's time to embody this transformation and become magnetic! In Part Two, as you embody the work you've done throughout this book so far, we'll be focusing on the flow state, how to flow with alignment, and how this can lead you to your aligned purpose. I'll guide you through this with my manifestation processes and the art of letting go.

By the end of Part Two, you'll feel magnetic, empowered and ready to step into an abundant brand new season of your life. You'll also be experiencing more flow and magnetism in your life as a whole and will begin to feel ready to welcome in your aligned abundance.

Flow, Don't Force

As I start to write this chapter, I'm in both a universal year 9 month and my own personal year 9 according to Numerology. In numerology, the number 9 symbolizes completion and endings. It also symbolizes the need for deep surrender and flowing with life as the old falls away. This really does reflect so much in my life currently. I initially feared this year 9, but as I settle into it, I'm realizing the true power and gift in surrendering and letting the old fall away. The energy of 9 allows us to let go of anything no longer serving us and to welcome in new beginnings. After all, without the endings, how could we start new journeys that will bring us aligned abundance?

This process of surrender invited me to deeply flow with life as I started a new chapter in my life, buying my first house and leaving my beloved old home where I'd lived for six years. All kinds of emotions came up, as I prepared to move out of the house that had changed everything for me. I knew, going into the house-buying journey, that it would call for deep surrender and the more I could step into flow, the easier it would be. This is what I've found in life, especially over the last few years now I've unpacked so much of my resistance through inner work. Today, as I trust and come from a grounded aligned energy, I don't fear, I don't feel worried and I trust deeply that the more I surrender, the more magic will enter my life.

I truly believe the level of magic in your life is a reflection of your ability to surrender. When we surrender our expectations, control or whatever it may be, we step out of our own way.

We allow the Universe to get to work and we align with our highest and brightest self. I've found that the more I relax into the manifestation process, the easier the journey has been and the more magic I've experienced within those manifestations.

Staying grounded and centred all of the time certainly can be hard when we experience the challenges of life. But when we approach each new situation with flow instead of resistance, we allow ourselves to be met by divine miracles and creative solutions. The more you challenge yourself to see beyond the obstacle or road block in your way, the more you create the space for flow.

Ease into a State of Flow

In a manifestation sense, flow state means being in the stream of abundance and feeling aligned with flow in all of its forms. You flow through life and feel a sense of flow and joy woven throughout your day. Random abundance flows to you through surrendered manifesting and trust. You release control and expectations, and allow yourself to flow and for your life to unfold in alignment with the Universe. Relaxing into flow state is one of the best things you can do for yourself throughout the manifesting journey, as you don't want to be the boulder blocking the stream of water in the river. You want to be the water flowing and moving with ease to your destination of aligned abundance.

So how do we get into a state of flow and experience this ease in life? When we try to force things or think we know better in the manifesting process, we create blocks, hurdles and rigidity, which – guess what – reflects right back to us! As I mentioned in chapter 12, flowing with the Universe requires divine surrender, trust and getting into flow state.

You've probably experienced flow state at some points during your manifestation journey, whether it be for a moment or a season in your life. We're always moving through moments of divine flow and what stops this is misalignment, rigidity and control, like in those unexpected moments when you're thrown into panic and try to take charge. Learning to regulate your nervous system in these moments allows you to ground back in and surrender to the flow of the situation.

Surrender and Let Go

Release the weight and burden you've been carrying by learning how to let go and surrender to the flow of life. When we cling on to our desires too tightly or attach to them, we weigh ourselves down with the burden of thinking we have to make things happen. Step 4 of letting go in my five-step manifesting process is arguably one of the most important steps, as it's then that we relax into receiving and co-creating with the Universe. Yet it's one of the least talked about steps in the manifestation sphere.

Your ability to tap into flow state depends on your ability to surrender and release your attachment to the outcome. Yet surrendering doesn't mean that you're giving up or that your desire won't happen; it's the opposite, actually. It means that you're okay with all outcomes and trust in the divine plan for your life ("this or something better for the highest good of all").

My favourite quote on surrender comes from the great Gabby Bernstein: "When you think you've surrendered surrender some more." When I first read this, I didn't get it. I understood I had to surrender, but how much surrendering could there be? Now, I repeat this quote as often as I can when leaning into surrender, as the deeper we surrender the more flow we experience. And the more flow we experience, the more aligned abundance and joy we get to experience in turn.

Letting go may look like letting go of any expectations of yourself or others, the past or even emotions that are no longer serving you. Challenge yourself to let go of control and surrender deeper into the knowing that it's safe to hand your concerns over to the Universe. Everything always works out and if it isn't okay, it's not the end.

Hand your attachments or fears over to the Universe and allow yourself to flow and be held by the divine. I often envision surrendering like floating in the ocean: if you struggle and kick around you're going to sink pretty quickly where you are; whereas if you allow yourself to float you're held and the current will take you to your destination so much quicker. It can be hard to kick back, relax and hand everything over to the Universe to steer, but remember that you can't see all the abundance and miracles waiting for you on the other side of surrender!

Aligned Abundance and Flow

Being able to go with the flow allows you to navigate unexpected situations, and it also allows miracles and abundance to flow to you. An example of this was a recent trip to Rome. I'd envisioned going to Rome to celebrate my 30th birthday in 2023, but after various work delays it just didn't end up happening. So I knew that 2024 would be the year we'd make it happen and we also planned to get engaged, to make the celebrations even more special.

However, my beloved grandad suddenly fell ill in the weeks leading up to our trip and I prayed he'd be okay while we were away. Sadly, the night before we were due to fly we got the call I never wanted to receive. My grandad had passed away and there we were, due to fly 12 hours later. Looking back on that evening, the flight was clearly divinely timed to allow me to process and grieve the night before we set off. All I could do was go with the flow and ride the wave of sorrow.

Our flight ended up being delayed by two hours and again I chose to surrender, in the knowledge that there was nowhere we needed to be and there was a divine reason for this. I was too busy processing my emotions even to care that we were late. When we arrived at our beautiful hotel, we were surprised to receive a room upgrade! It was my first ever room upgrade manifestation and after the 24 hours I'd just had, I was very grateful for the Universe supporting me and making sure the trip was special.

Throughout our four days in Rome, we had to go with the flow when it came to travel and the weather. It'd been forecast to rain on the morning of the proposal, yet I kept saying to myself and my partner, Alex, "The Universe wouldn't let us go through all of this to have our engagement rained off." I set the intention for blue clear skies and – guess what? – against all odds it was sunny! On the morning of our engagement, we arrived as Alex had planned at 7:15am at the Colosseum to bright, blue skies – only for the gate to be locked to the park where he wanted to propose! Alex and our amazing photographer, Lidia, were both panicking, but going with the flow once more, I just said, "Let's do the photoshoot first and then come back and do the proposal afterwards. I trust there's a reason why the gate is locked." So we went and had some beautiful photos taken around Rome, and when we came back the gate was open! By this point, it had gone cloudy but as any avid photographer knows cloudy skies make the best lighting.

The important lesson here is that through divine surrender and trust, the most magical things happened for us, including a luxury room upgrade and our beautiful engagement photographs. I would have loved for my grandad to have seen us get engaged, but I'm certain he was with us in Rome celebrating all the same. We can't control what happens to us in life or when unexpected situations will arise but through the power of flowing and divine trust the most amazing abundance can flow to you as you allow yourself to flow with the situation.

Choose Alignment and Flow

Back in January of 2024, I made sure to write down everything that happened, so you could see exactly what happened when, despite everything, I chose alignment and flow. I could tell I was in flow state by the way these opportunities unfolded – and they can for you, too, when you make aligned flowing choices!

Around the same time, I was hosting my sixth annual free five-day manifesting event, with over 3,000 of you, so it was safe to say I was in flow state and in the vortex of creating aligned abundance momentum. My goal for the year was to say no to more things and to say yes only to things that truly felt aligned.

To kick-start this process of alignment, an old friend popped up who'd been talking about planning a night away somewhere for over two years! In the past, I'd have said, "Yes, that sounds great. When are you free?" Then I wouldn't hear back for over six months, when she'd ask again and the cycle would repeat. Well, a lot had changed in both our lives over the past two years and as we barely spoke anymore, it just didn't feel right to keep entertaining this cycle and saying yes. So when my friend reached out again, I changed my answer to, "I'm not able to commit to this at the moment, but I'd love to have a catch-up on the phone when you're free?"

Once again, I didn't hear back, but by reclaiming my power and not saying yes when really the answer was a no, within half an hour I had an email from Primark offering me a huge opportunity to be their "manifestation expert" on their socials and podcast. I told my friend Hannah what had happened and she said, "See what happens! When you say no to things that don't align, the real alignment can come in!" So we put this further to the test.

The very next day, a peer reached out to me and asked me to do a mastermind workshop. As I didn't know this person very well and knew she was teaching people how to be seven-figure coaches in this mastermind course of hers, for which she was charging handsomely, I asked if I would receive a fee for the workshop. After all, I normally charge for this type of in-depth training and would expect my peers to charge me in turn if I asked to use their time, energy and expertise on one of my own platforms.

What happened next truly shocked me. I received a voice note back laughing and mocking me. I was told how I was expected to do this for free to help them out, even though my knowledge was clearly worth something to this person. Again, if it had been a friend I would have considered it, but being laughed at showed me how little this person walked their talk or respected me. So I politely said the dates didn't align and I wasn't the right person for the mastermind. The very same day, on the New Moon in Capricorn (11/1), Watkins offered me this book deal. It suddenly snapped into place and aligned!

Finally, during the course of my week-long experiment with flow, I was asked to speak at an event at the last minute. While it looked great, the organizers were asking me to bend over backward and wanted me to lower my fee. While I'll always try to make something work, as I know what it's like when running my own events, all of the hassle and what would be an eight-hour trip for a 45-minute talk was a hell no, especially at such short notice. So I politely declined and didn't hear back. The very same day, my mum sent me a picture of my book *Hurt, Healing, Healed* on display in a large store here in the UK. I'd Photoshopped an image of that book on the shelf of a big book store and I'd placed it on my vision board only 11 days prior and, just like that, it'd manifested!

You can see by my flow experiment, how when I started saying no to the things that no longer aligned with me (and which I would have said yes to in the past out of fear and people pleasing), amazing manifestations began to come in effortlessly! By clearing out the so-called opportunities that weren't for me and would have zapped my joy, the most aligned opportunities could manifest. Now, I know that saying no to what looks like great opportunities isn't always easy and I've definitely doubted myself in the past about whether I'm making the right decision, but when you make an aligned choice that will bring you joy over money or whatever it is, you can never go wrong. Every time I say no, I trust that better is always aligning – and it really is!

Creating this ripple of abundance in your life is simple: the tools in this book will help you create the vortex of flow and momentum and now it's your turn to start saying no when you really mean no, and to say YASS only to those things that truly align with you and feel expansive. If it takes you further away from your joy or your desire, then it's not in alignment for you. Trust that in your aligned no, your aligned YASS will bring bigger and better, baby!

Go with the Flow

A big part of my writing process is about honouring my flow. There's nothing that'll trigger writer's block more than forcing yourself to write a chapter or push through when it's just not flowing. And it's the same with any project or task in life: it's never going to be your best work if you force your way to inspiration and motivation.

It's important to acknowledge when it's time to stop, reset, realign and pivot. Is your current task or project flowing effortlessly? Or do you find yourself staring at your computer screen, for example, and getting easily distracted, just hoping that divine inspiration will eventually strike?

When we force ourselves to complete a task or project even when it's not flowing, we're slipping into control mode. Now, deadlines of course don't always help our flow; while for some a deadline helps them to focus and be held accountable, for others who are perhaps more intuitive with their work, no matter how many deadlines they have, if it isn't flowing they won't complete it. As with anything, balance is key here – for me, if my writing isn't flowing, I move onto a different project that is. I honour my flow and where my energy feels drawn to go. If I have a deadline and the inspiration isn't flowing, I will put it down to focus on what does feel good and then come back to it the next day if I can, or another day that feels more in alignment. Without fail, the inspiration and motivation flow as I honour what wants to flow through me and into my life.

When we're rigid with our work or flow, we become the very block in the river stopping the natural flow of water from reaching its destination. When we honour our flow in productivity and motivation, we channel our energy into whichever projects or tasks do feel in alignment to us at that given time, which of course creates more alignment in our life. Another point to consider when forcing a task or project is whether this relaxes your nervous system ... or is forcing it actually causing stress within your body?

The secret to creativity and, in my experience, channelling your best work and talents lies in honouring your flow and where your energy wants to go. If you can put down that project that feels rigid right now and stuck, please do! Use this time to reset the energy, pivot if necessary and realign with where your energy is flowing and feeling aligned. Set up time in your schedule to look at it again in two days' time or a week, depending on your timescale. For those of you who are panicking because you have to do that thing today, carve out the time to set yourself up for success. Cultivate the most flowing environment for yourself and ask the Universe to bring flow and inspiration into your project or task. Two great mantras I love repeating when I feel overwhelmed or stressed are:

"There is always enough time for the things that matter to me."
and
"I invite divine flow into my day and tasks."

Maybe it's not a task or project you feel stuck in; maybe it's bigger than that and it concerns a particular area of your life or the season of life that you're currently in. If that applies to you then gratitude is the quickest way to tap back into flow state when you're feeling frustrated or stuck. How can you express gratitude and appreciation for all you have here and now?

When you switch your attitude to gratitude, you open up the floodgates for flow to pour into your life, as you tap back into the present moment and give thanks for your current blessings. Take, for example, that job you really hate, so you're desperate to manifest your dream job; well, it won't manifest until there's flow to your current job, much as you dislike it. However, your situation can be transformed through the power of gratitude. How lucky are you to have a job that pays your bills in full and on time? How lucky are you to have a job that pays for your home and transport? Even if it's one positive in an overall negative situation, draw upon what you've learned – including how lucky you are to know what you don't want in a job!

Avoid Self-Sabotage

The other day, my friend reminded me of the saying "waiting for the other shoe to drop", meaning waiting for something to happen that we feel is inevitable. This is one of the most common fears we all share, when we start to fear what could go wrong. Parents experience it as they stare at their precious newborns and worry that something bad may happen to them. That underlying anxiety is there, too, when we say things like, "Surely it can't get better than this?" or "Surely I can't get that lucky – what's going to happen next?" Please let me reassure you that we're conditioned as humans to fear the worst and worry.

The truth is we all have these thoughts, especially if we had a troubled upbringing, experienced poverty, homelessness or other extreme traumas growing up. When you finally do create stability and safety in your life, guess what? Your subconscious mind will remind you of how you could lose it all again. The connecting fear here is loss.

As I started to manifest my wildest dreams and hugely up-level my life, self-sabotage started to make itself known to me. Any time something positive or amazing happened, I'd feel incredible, then think, "What if I lose this too?" and "What if it doesn't last?" Or, "If something big like this has happened, what bad thing will happen in my life to bring me back down?" Maybe you can relate to these sorts of thoughts yourself. Whether self-sabotage looks like loss, fear or even subtle self-sabotage like setting a health goal and then eating all your favourite unhealthy meals, it shows up for us all in varying degrees and can be part of the habits we form in response to our upbringing and childhood conditioning.

It's taken a lot of flow and surrender along my journey to relax and settle into the goodness in my life; I honour the journey I've been on and why my nervous system and mind react the way they do when blessings do come into my life. Remember that our nervous system and subconscious mind are programmed to keep us safe, so despite self-sabotage seeming negative, it's actually only ever trying to protect us. And how can we be mad at our beautiful body for protecting us after all it's been through? I want to challenge you to think about how can you reframe your self-sabotage into gratitude and give thanks for your incredible intelligent body protecting you. Be gentle with yourself, too. Show compassion and love for yourself during acts of self-sabotage, as it's important to acknowledge why it's coming up and also how you can break this habit and pattern for good and show your nervous system and inner child that it's safe to receive and safe to surrender to the flow of life.

Remove Blocks to Flow

Don't be the boulder blocking the flow of water. And remember that the only block when it comes to flow is yourself. Are your flowing or are you forcing? Are you flowing in the direction the Universe wants to take you, or are you fighting the current and trying to go upstream? Remember what is meant for you will always fall into place.

A common way we can end up being the boulder blocking flow and abundance in our life is through people pleasing. Our intuition is a powerful inner compass and when we don't listen to those niggles, nudges and gut feelings, we go against the flow and can end up blocking ourselves. I know from previous experiences when I've gone against the flow and pushed forward with something and ignored my intuition, things always fall apart. Something comes up, another red flag appears, things even get cancelled, or sometimes I've realized it's my time to walk away. When we're people pleasing or ignoring our intuition, we're becoming the boulder; the Universe won't intervene (due to our human free will), so it's down to us to realize we're the one stopping the flow and to get out of our own way. Think now about how you might be stopping the flow of abundance in your life or with your manifestation? Where are you fighting against the flow? Even if you can't see an obvious block right now, invite yourself to surrender more to flow and allow miracles into this situation. How can you let go and allow the Universe to flow with you once again?

You can also end up blocking flow by questioning the Universe. For example, if you're questioning the signs that the Universe is sending your way, this itself is a clear sign of a lack of trust. As we covered in chapter 8, "Trust the Universe", trust and belief must come from within yourself first. If you're questioning the clarity of any signs you receive, then make sure to revisit the prompts and aligned actions in that chapter to deepen your flow with the Universe. The Universe wants to deliver your beautiful messages and signs, and this is why I always suggest letting them flow to you without seeking them out! That way, you're not controlling them or needing to see them, so when you do see them you know it's a clear divine sign that the Universe is communicating with you, as there were no expectations on your part to receive a sign. So if you've been using signs or synchronicities as an emotional crutch on which to build belief, put the signs down and allow yourself to flow with the Universe.

Keep Going With the Flow

Unexpected moments in our day can throw us off course and make our nervous system spiral into stress and panic. The fact is that we can never predict life's uncertainties, nor can we be exempt from them. As much as we are the creators of our reality, life isn't just black and white. There is more at play here for, as we know, the Law of Attraction is only one of seven energetic laws here in this Universe. Meaning we all experience moments where we're required to surrender our control and go with the flow. If you're someone who struggles with change or feels anxiety in unexpected moments or problems, then learning to regulate and flow will help you to ground in and be present in these moments.

After completing the previous Aligned Actions in this book, you may have found that you're naturally surrendering and going with the flow more now than you used to. Nature can also help you to connect to flow, whether that's through water or by grounding yourself into the Earth. Mother Nature is the true essence of flow and by connecting to her and the water elementals (i.e. nature spirits), you can embody the energy of flow and surrender in your life. If you have a body of water near you such as the ocean, a lake, a pond or even a waterfall, I'd encourage you to go and sit by this and notice how your energy changes as you tune in to the water and flow.

One of my favourite things to do at the beach is to stand in the ocean and ask the water elementals (such as the energy of mermaids as they are connected to emotions and relationships) to wash away any blocks to flow or emotions I'm holding on to. With each wave crashing in and out over my feet and legs, I visualize that they are washing the energy away from me and helping me to flow. Give this a try for yourself and see how you feel afterwards!

Aligned Actions

Action

I want you to take a moment to reflect on each area of your life (see the list below) and journal about your observations around flow in your notebook or journal. In what areas do you find yourself able to flow easily and in what areas of your life do you struggle to go with the flow? Use the prompts below to help you dive deeper into your relationship with flow and explore why you may feel unable to fully flow in these areas of your life currently.

- relationships/significant other
- money/finances
- health
- career
- purpose
- spirituality

Do any of your answers surprise you?

Intention

Over the next four weeks, I want you to keep a flow diary in your journal or notebook. At the end of each week, I'd like you to answer these four questions and keep yourself accountable with your flow journey. Stick to this intentional practice over these four weeks, as your flow diary will provide valuable insights into how you can tap into flow more often and also be a record of the abundance that flows to you as a result.

- How have I gone with the flow this week?
- How have I not gone with the flow this week?
- How did it feel to lean into surrendering more – what came up?
- What unexpected abundance or surprises came my way this week as a result?

If you'd like to take your flow journey deeper than I recommend listening to my "Flow, Release and Surrender" meditation which is available via my website in the *Aligned Abundance* meditation playlist. You can find a handy link for this in the resources at the back of this book.

Journaling Prompts

- How do I react to unexpected situations?
- Why do I feel I respond in this way?
- How could I respond differently to these unexpected situations?
- What tools can I use to regulate my nervous system in these moments?
- What stops me from being in flow state consistently?
- How can I tap into flow state more this week?
- How can I flow more with life?

ALIGNED REFLECTIONS

- The level of magic in your life is a reflection of your ability to surrender.
- The more you challenge yourself to see beyond the obstacle or road block in your way, the more you create the space for flow.
- You don't want to be the boulder blocking the stream of water in the river. You want to be the water flowing and moving with ease to your destination of aligned abundance.
- Your ability to tap into a state of flow depends on your ability to surrender and release attachment.
- It can be hard to kick back, relax and hand things over to the Universe to steer, but remember that you can't see all the abundance and miracles waiting for you on the other side of surrender!
- We can't control what happens to us in life or when unexpected situations will arise, but through the power of flowing and divine trust the most amazing abundance can flow to you as you allow yourself to flow with the situation.
- Trust that in your aligned no, your aligned YASS will bring bigger and better, baby!
- It's never going to be your best work if you force your way to inspiration and motivation.
- If you've been using signs or synchronicities as an emotional crutch, put the signs down and allow yourself to flow with the Universe.

Alignment and New Seasons

The secret to aligned abundance is knowing that your alignment will change from moment to moment and from season to season. As you can hopefully see by now, you'll know you're in alignment by the way it feels and by the way it makes your body and nervous system feel. For example, this morning, on the way back from the beach, I realized I haven't felt in alignment this week. Instead of getting upset about this, I remembered it's okay because I've been navigating a lot recently and however long it may last, feeling out of alignment in this season of my life means that I can be sure to embody the very tools that will allow me to write the most aligned book possible for you.

We can't help which way the wind will blow for us in life, but we can change the sails of our boat to find alignment with the conditions we're experiencing. This is why regular check-ins with yourself and your desires, followed by pivots where necessary, are the secret sauce to alignment – because how will you truly know if you're not in alignment with something unless you sit down and spend time with it? So often we can get so busy with life and immersed in what's out of alignment just in order to keep on going, that we end up not feeling great and maybe our habits, rituals and self-care go out the window, too. When we slow down and create the space to look at why we don't feel truly in alignment within ourselves and with our desires, we can create shifts, miracles and changes. You may even realize that in this season of your life alignment looks a little different, as you navigate loss, grief or other challenges – and that's okay as well.

I mentioned in chapter 10 how I use the seasons of the year as an opportunity to check in with myself and my manifestations, and the same can apply to the seasons of your life. During these mini check-ins I look at my daily practice, what's feeling joyful and expansive in my life and what's not. I then use this important feedback from my soul as an invitation to make changes, realign and take inspired action toward the feelings and reality I do want. These regular check-ins and pivots are non-negotiable to me now, as I see how magnetic they make me to up-levelling and also to aligned abundance.

Some people spend months or even years feeling stuck or stagnant and it might take a big wake-up call for them to realize they're not in alignment and need to make a change. Don't be that person; remember that your desires want you, too, and now you have the tools and awareness in your life to make yourself and your desires a priority every season. That's all it takes: once every week, month or even every three months, spend time intentionally with your soul and make sure your practices, rituals and intentions still feel in alignment and feel good to you. If they don't, you can then make the necessary changes to pivot and realign as necessary.

Recently, a lovely lady in my Manifestation Membership shared that she felt upset as she hadn't dedicated enough time to the tasks and activities connected to flow, to which I replied, "Maybe not doing everything was you going with the flow and really embodying flow as you listened to your body and your energy!" The same works with alignment: it doesn't have to make sense to anyone other than yourself. When we get distracted by what others are doing and especially when we find ourselves doing things because we feel we have to, we zap the joy and alignment from ourselves so quickly.

Find Your Purpose

As you navigate new seasons of your life, your alignment, definition of wealth and even your sense of purpose may change. I often get asked, "How do you find your purpose?" After sitting down with some of the most inspiring people in the world on my podcast, I've come to realize our purpose isn't one thing and nor is our alignment. Our purpose, alignment and joy all come from moments. Moments that grow, change and evolve as we grow, change and evolve.

Your purpose in your twenties could be to travel the world and help incredible organizations in other countries. Your purpose in your thirties could then change to caring for an elderly or ill relative. We never have just the one purpose in life, although we may have a main purpose per season of our life. Maybe right now your purpose is to feel uncertain about what's next and this season is for you to find yourself, grow and serve yourself. Whatever form it takes, everyone's purpose is beautifully needed in this world and will change throughout their life.

I certainly don't expect my purpose to stay the same throughout my lifetime. Even if I just look back 10 years, my purpose then was to help people get out of debt and use coupons. Never did I think that a decade later I would writing my fourth manifestation book and helping people manifest their wildest dreams!

When people don't evolve with their purpose, they can start to feel stuck or stagnant. They don't understand why their beloved job, hobby or purpose doesn't feel expansive anymore and they can become stuck for years or even decades in their familiar comfort zones and through fear of taking that leap. Our purpose is here to challenge us and when we learn everything we need to in a season of our life, a new season will unfold – one that requires a new version of ourselves, a new alignment, a new purpose. This new season may look similar to the previous season or take you somewhere completely different.

For example, when I look at my alignment last year, it felt all over the place, as I went through my year 9 in numerology (which relates to endings). Besides this, as I've mentioned, deep childhood trauma that I'd no prior awareness of came up for me, my partner and I moved into our first home together, and I started writing this very book. This year, my alignment has looked hugely different. For me, here in 2024 as I'm writing this, it's now a year 1 in numerology, we got engaged and are now planning our wedding, I'm wrapping up this book and the projects and exciting things I've birthed this year have felt so magical and joyful because of the hard work I did last year. Neither year was bad or good, nor in alignment or out of alignment per se, although I needed to draw upon my tools more last year than this year.

We all go through these ebbs and flows of life. Some seasons will feel easier and some seasons will be stormier, but grounding in, tapping in to your spiritual toolkit and trusting deeply in this season of your life and where it's taking you are vital for your alignment journey.

Alignment isn't a Destination

When I tell people about aligned abundance, many tell me that they deeply want to feel in alignment again but they don't know how – they just have a deep yearning. This desire or yearning is your soul craving lightness, fun, joy and expansiveness once again. Although alignment is a journey rather than a destination, it's also a by-product of creating those emotions and feelings that you do want to experience in life, whether that's more joy or happiness, for example.

Alignment doesn't come out of nowhere; it comes as a result of listening to your body and your soul, and creating the catalyst for joy and happiness in your life. Then you will experience flow and alignment as you align with this season of your life. Listening to your alignment, flow and purpose in each season is key to navigating the inevitable ups and downs of life; this will allow you to create a solid emotional foundation that will support you when you need to rely on it more.

Everything in your life has purpose – from your friendships, hobbies and work, to your family life and especially your relationship with yourself. Often we confuse purpose with our life's work and while for some that is true, our purpose runs more deeply than simply what we choose to get paid for in this lifetime. Our purpose is our soul mission here on Earth; it's about what our soul chooses to learn, embody and serve within this lifetime. Often, purpose can take the form of a service-based role through which we leave the world better than when we found it. For some, their purpose may be to be a world leader and create huge change for people, while for others, their purpose may be to be the friendly face at the corner shop who becomes a staple in their community and supports the locals. Every purpose is equally important and yours will absolutely find you. However, if you're struggling to find your purpose in this season of your life, then here are some tips and tools.

Define Your Purpose

Start off by defining what purpose means to you here and now; for example, does it mean the work you're paid to do, or something else that lights you up or adds value and meaning to your life? Everyone's answer will be different and change over time, so tune in to what purpose means for you here and now. Your purpose can be fluid and whatever you want it to be.

Follow the Breadcrumbs

Once you've set the intention to manifest your purpose or for it to reveal itself to you, the Universe will absolutely start leaving you signs, synchronicities and breadcrumbs to follow on your path toward it. Notice the nudges from the Universe and explore these options and opportunities with an open mind. Try any opportunities that arise and see which ones resonate with you and which ones don't. Then you'll have a clearer sense of what feels in alignment for you.

Remember, Every Experience is Part of Your Purpose

Don't knock your past experiences; just like with my couponing business, it served a particular purpose in that season of your life and is all part of your wider purpose. For me, running that business taught me so many valuable tools, skills and business knowledge, which set me up for success with my spiritual work today. Everything is leading you to where you are now, so I would encourage you to write down in your journal or notebook what valuable skills or tools you've learned through your previous roles or passions.

What Lights You Up?

What do you feel drawn to do in this season of your life? Are there any passions or hobbies you really want to try? Your purpose won't always equate to a source of income, so if you're happy and fulfilled in your job but still feel drawn to a deeper sense of purpose, then your purpose might lie elsewhere right now. Think about what lights you up and brings a sense of purpose to your life. Is there something that really lights you up that you'd love to share with the world? One question that I believe is the key to discovering your alignment and purpose in this season of your life is this: "If I were to die tomorrow, what is one thing I'd be sad I didn't birth, do or create?" Journal upon this now and whatever your answer is, this is your clue for where to start. Follow those breadcrumbs and see where your journey takes you.

Alignment and Overwhelm

I was working with a lovely lady in a 1-to-1 session recently, when she shared with me that she felt out of alignment due to always being busy and self-sabotaging her spiritual practices. Every time she found time to do them, she'd make an excuse to keep herself busy. This is a very common story when it comes to alignment, so please let me remind you that manifestation should feel fun!

If you resonate with this client's story, you may feel mentally exhausted because you're doing too much. I feel this too when I'm busying myself and coping in a stressful period. However, I know that when I slow down and surrender, I stop resisting and those feelings of overwhelm disappear. Coming back into alignment in this case means creating spaciousness in your day and in your life to slow down, reset and check in with what you've been avoiding (see chapter 5). We busy ourselves to stop ourselves from slowing down, whether that's to avoid confronting uncomfortable feelings or because we don't want uncomfortable thoughts to come back up. But as we know, what we resist persists and the energy of resistance will only sabotage our inner alignment and block our aligned abundance.

Overwhelm can also look like feeling overwhelmed by not knowing what your purpose is or what this season of life is for. I actually think sometimes it's okay not to know. Try not to worry; instead, just remember that it's in the quietness and spaciousness that we get our biggest downloads of information and inspiration, which will help us know what our next aligned action should be. So if you're unsure, get still, slow down and take yourself out of the situations that are keeping you distracted and trapped in a loop of feeling out of alignment.

THREE TYPES OF ALIGNMENT

Before we look at some signs of alignment, I quickly want to remind you of the three types of alignment that I mentioned in chapter 1. Don't forget either that each season of our life will require a different type of alignment and energy from us.

Daily alignment: focuses on the choices and micro decisions we make daily and change frequently to bring joy and purpose into our day. These create the foundation for an overall feeling of alignment in our life. Your day-to-day micro decisions start to add up to the seasonal and soul alignment.

Seasonal alignment: the actual or metaphysical season of life you're currently in. These decisions impact things like our sense of purpose and our life choices. They can affect us for months or years and will change with the passage of time.

Soul Alignment: concerns the grand scheme of your life and the wider collective. These are long-term soul desires that you feel a deep sense of alignment with and while these can change and evolve over time, they feel more lasting.

Signs of Alignment

Throughout this book, I've shared tools and techniques to help you identify when something is out of alignment. Now, as we journey into this new chapter of aligned abundance in your life, I want to describe some signs from the Universe that may appear to show that you're on the right path.

Angel Numbers

If you keep seeing repeating numbers like 222, 333, 777 or 11:11 appear in your life, this is a sign that your angels are communicating with you. Whenever I see the number 444, for example, I know it's my angels communicating with me "all is well". There are a whole multitude of definitions around angel numbers online and it's easy to get confused when there are so many meanings for the same number. This is why I've started to tune in to what I feel when I see them. When I see 444, I feel a sense of calm, peace and the knowing that all is well (or all is aligned for me). I now understand this to be my angels' way of reassuring me and letting me know I'm on the right path. So if you see repeating numbers in your day-to-day life, tune in and ask what they mean, although you can of course look them up online and see which definition resonates with you, too. You can also pick another sign (like an animal, object or a colour) and set an intention for the Universe to show you this sign when you're on the right path.

Flow

As we spoke about in the last chapter, when you're on the right path, things will just effortlessly flow. Aligned opportunities will pour in and any stuck or stagnant projects will all of a sudden flow and get completed! You'll feel surrendered, flowing and open as you align with the Universe and divine flow in your life. As you flow, aligned abundance will effortlessly flow into your life, too.

"Winks" from the Universe

When I'm flowing and in alignment, I notice how the Universe will send winks in the form of people, conversations and abundance. I might be debating a decision and a friend will mention a specific word or topic that gives me that final nudge to say yes or no. Or I might see a sign on an advert or billboard that instantly makes me feel clear in my mind around a decision. The Universe is always there, holding our hand along this journey of life, and once you keep an eye out for them yourself, you will definitely spot these winks from the Universe in small and big ways.

Magnetism

Another clear sign of alignment in your life is your magnetism. You will feel utterly magnetic to abundance of all kinds, and new opportunities and joy will appear seemingly out of nowhere. You will feel a sense of magnetism as your desires align effortlessly and you may even notice unexpected abundance pour in, too. Life will feel easy and you'll feel like a true manifestation magnet!

New Beginnings

As I begin to wrap up this magnetic journey with you, I've been struggling to know how to end such a potent chapter on purpose and, of course, finish this beloved book and journey I've so loved going on with you. Something just didn't feel quite in alignment, shall we say ... It dawned on me last night, as I told my fiancé how I was struggling to finish this chapter, that I actually did know how to end it and my experiences over the last few weeks had shown me what alignment and new seasons really feel like.

I've recently ended some old cycles of emotional pain in an area of my life, which has been huge for me; even my body has been purging this recently, as I've stepped into this new season of new beginnings, new cycles and the unknown. It felt strange to let this die away in my life and turn to nothing, but this is actually exactly what needed to happen. I knew that in order to experience this new season of alignment, I needed to let the old die away and the ultimate reset to happen from fresh energy, a fresh perspective and, most importantly, a surrendered state.

In this new season of my life, it definitely feels like I'm entering the unknown; but that is the beauty of new seasons: we don't know how they'll pan out. It's just like when we start watching a great TV series, and we have no idea what the characters will go through or how the story will unfold, but it's exciting because we're going on the journey with them and learning about the show. This energy of curiosity and openness creates the catalyst for new possibilities to unfold. In the same way, when we step into a new season of alignment, we get to meet a brand new version of ourselves and may even meet the very abundance we've been trying to manifest. Manifestations can only come in these new seasons; that's the beauty of them – that with every ending comes a beautiful new cycle of beginnings where aligned abundance awaits.

When you hit the reset button, new energy and new possibilities can unfold in your life. It's in the nothingness, in the dark fertile soil of possibility, that the new seed can start to burst through the soil and bloom into the manifestation you've been seeking.

So are you gripping too tightly to this old season? Are you holding on to those previous identities of yours and old comforts in order to stay safe? Or are you ready to lay it all down, hit the reset button and walk into this new cycle and season of your life? If you picked up this book because you've been feeling out of alignment, chances are you are in fact ready to put the past down and welcome in this new beginning and season. So loosen your grip, release those expectations and allow yourself to flow effortlessly with the unknown and the infinite possibilities and aligned abundance that comes with this.

I want to end this chapter with a few words I'd written down but couldn't find the right place for, until now. And of course, as if by divine alignment, the Universe knew they were meant to be shared here ...

Release comes at the specific time we find deep acceptance of what was, what is and what will never be. Express gratitude for what was and all the lessons and blessings it gave you. But it's time to put this down and step into a new season of life and possibility.

Aligned Actions

Action

Head to the resources for this book at www.emmamumford. co.uk/alignedabundance to access my "New Beginnings and Embodiment" meditation, which is designed to help you embody your healing journey throughout this book and to step powerfully into this new abundant season of your life. Journal down any messages or symbols that come through in the meditation.

Intention

As your last intentional action in this book, I want you to think about your purpose in this season of your life and whether your purpose lies in your job (i.e. how you earn money) or something different. Reflect on your current job and see whether you are fulfilled there or whether you've outgrown this purpose. If you don't like your job, then this is a big sign to re-evaluate and ask yourself whether it's in alignment with who you are here and now. Use the journaling prompts below to help you to dive deeper into this.

Journaling Prompts

- What is my purpose in this season of my life?
- Where am I feeling overwhelmed in my life?
- If I were to die tomorrow, what is one thing I'd be sad I didn't birth, do or create?

- What lights me up in life?
- How has my purpose changed and evolved over the years?
- What new beginning am I now stepping into?

ALIGNED REFLECTIONS

- We can't help which way the wind will blow for us in life, but we can change the sails of our boat to find alignment with the conditions we're experiencing.
- Our purpose, alignment and joy all come from moments. Moments that grow, change and evolve as we grow, change and evolve.
- Our purpose is here to challenge us and when we learn everything we need to in a season of our life, a new season will unfold – one that requires a new version of ourselves, a new alignment, a new purpose. And that season may look similar to the previous season or take you somewhere completely new.
- Alignment doesn't come first, it comes as a result of listening to your body and to your soul, and creating the catalyst for joy and happiness in your life.
- Listening to your alignment, flow and purpose in each season is key to navigating the inevitable ups and downs of life. Through this, you'll create a solid emotional foundation that will support you when you need to rely on them more.
- Our purpose is our soul mission here on Earth – what our soul chooses to learn, embody and serve with in this lifetime.
- It's in the quietness and spaciousness that we get our biggest downloads of information and inspiration, which tells us what our next aligned action is.
- Manifestations can only come in these new seasons; that's the beauty of them: that with every ending comes a beautiful new cycle of beginnings where aligned abundance awaits.
- Loosen your grip, release those expectations and allow yourself to flow effortlessly with the unknown and the infinite possibilities and aligned abundance that come with this.

The Alignment
Path Ahead

As we wrap up our time together here in *Aligned Abundance*, I want to take this opportunity to remind you again that alignment is a journey, not a destination, and that this book will serve you as a guide for life in those seasons where you may feel out of sorts or stuck. Throughout our time together, we've gone deep into the many layers of alignment, your soul and its wisdom. I hope you've enjoyed reconnecting with your soul and your truth, and meeting the authentic version of yourself. My vision for this book was to guide you through a deep process of unravelling any pushing, forcing and control around manifestation and show you that it gets to be easy; your desires want you too and when you operate from a place of power (i.e. authenticity), magic, abundance and alignment are available to you and your manifestations will feel effortless and aligned!

As you read these final pages, I hope you feel a sense of achievement, flow and peace for all that you've accomplished. I also hope you'll look back at the aligned abundance intention that you wrote back in the Introduction and see progress, shifts or even the materialization of your manifestation in your reality! My wish is that as you've leaned into each chapter, you've been able to meet a new version of yourself and release any masks or identities that have been hiding your beautiful light from the world. I'd like for you to have a sense of being at home within yourself and to feel unwavering trust and faith in the Universe and the divine plan for your life. I also hope you've been able to embody new positive identities and release any that were stopping the flow of abundance and magic in your life, and I hope more than anything your *Aligned Abundance* journey has helped you to remember that manifesting gets to be fun and joyful! If you don't feel all of the energy that I've described here, don't worry; Rome wasn't built in a day and this is your alignment journey, during which alignment will look and feel different in each season of your life.

When writing my books, I always go on the adventure with you, as I learn these lessons and embody them to be able to share these tools and wisdom with you. When I reflect on this book, which really started to take shape back in 2021 when creating my course, I see the magic, alignment and magnetism that have unfolded for me since then. I look at my life with awe when I see how much bliss, alignment and happiness have flowed into it as I've embodied my own aligned abundance. This is why I'm so excited for you to do this work – and hopefully you can already see these powerful shifts in your own reality.

When Watkins gave me my deadline back in January 2024, I honestly didn't know *how* I would write an entire book in that time. I often joke that writing a book is like birthing a baby and when writing you do feel energetically pregnant, so to speak. Now, as I prepare to write these final words and hand this book over to the Universe and to the editors, I think it's no coincidence that this journey has taken me nine months – just like the many cycles and seasons I mention within these pages.

I hope that you, too, have experienced the magic and flow that have been woven into this book with so much love for you. I want you to have experienced flow, shifts, joy and abundance as you've dived into the aligned actions and prompts. Throughout these pages, I've shared with you my alignment process and a deeper look into what alignment is and why it's essential in the manifestation process; moving forward, these teachings will allow you to navigate seasons of feeling stuck, out of alignment and your desires feeling blocked. It's all about alignment and what you're in line with!

It has been my absolute honour to be your guide to aligned abundance and really this isn't goodbye, as it's simply the beginning of your beautiful alignment process that you'll continue to move into throughout your life. My aim is for you to eventually not even need this book, but of course if you wish to revisit your favourite chapters, tools or prompts then of course they will be there for you whenever you want to realign, pivot and shift.

Which brings me nicely to our first check-in point together – my alignment protocol that you first read about in chapter 1. Reflect on how you've moved through this process throughout the book and how you can use this protocol in the future to help you identify when something is feeling out of alignment in your life.

MY ALIGNMENT PROTOCOL

1. **Stop:** If it was aligned, it would be flowing. If a manifestation, project or even relationship feels like an uphill struggle, doors keep closing and you're experiencing endless frustration no matter how much work you do, it's time to stop and reassess your alignment with this situation.
2. **Reset:** If something is feeling out of alignment, it's time to reset the energy, as old ways won't open new doors. How can you reset the energy of this situation energetically and with your actions?
3. **Realign:** How can you reframe this situation? What is the opportunity being presented here from the Universe? Reframe the situation and use this as an opportunity to come into alignment with yourself, your priorities and move forward from a new state of alignment and flow.

Our next check-in is to see how you've moved through the two pillars of alignment. Throughout this book we've journeyed through both of these steps, so I invite you to spend some time reflecting on how you feel within yourself now that you're starting to experience alignment within yourself and to know the authentic version of yourself. What have you been able to embody throughout your *Aligned Abundance* journey?

TWO PILLARS OF MANIFESTATION ALIGNMENT

PILLAR #1: ALIGNMENT WITHIN YOURSELF

Coming into alignment in life requires you to come into alignment within yourself first. This can look like:

- aligning within your mind, body and spirit
- reconnecting
- grounding back in
- discovering and expressing your authentic self
- strengthening your intuition
- honouring your body
- making aligned decisions – decisions that match your own values
- knowing when to walk away from what's no longer serving you and keeping you stuck

PILLAR #2: ALIGNMENT WITH YOUR DESIRE

Once you're experiencing alignment internally, this can now be reflected into the outer world through flow, abundance and aligning with the version of yourself who is a match for your desire. This can look like:

- flowing over forcing
- embodying the emotions and feelings of your desired outcome
- becoming the version of yourself who has your desire through embodiment practices that will help magnetize your new reality to you
- taking aligned and inspired action to meet the Universe halfway
- surrendering to the divine plan for your life

I want you to witness how incredible you truly are for picking up this book, committing to the practices, reading every page and now completing it! Your future self is already thanking you for doing this work and for expressing your true beautiful self. I'd love to invite you to do a check-in with me now to see how far you've come and reflect on the shifts you've experienced. Journal on these final prompts below in your journal or notebook ...

- What has been my biggest takeaway throughout this journey?
- What does aligned abundance mean to me?
- What shifts or abundance have I manifested throughout this book?
- What would I like to work on, moving forward?
- How has my abundance mindset shifted since reading this book?
- How do I feel toward my desires now I'm at the end of this book?
- What does my highest timeline look and feel like?
- What is one thing I'm really proud of myself for achieving during my *Aligned Abundance* journey?
- How do I plan to celebrate myself this week?

I'm so pleased for you, Queen, and so proud of you for saying yes to yourself, your aligned abundance and your desires! As you're journaling on these reflections, I hope you, too, can see just how much progress and many shifts you've manifested since our work together began. And the best bit is the fun doesn't stop here! Now you have the awareness, the tools and the knowledge you need to let aligned abundance flow into your life, you can create these very feelings in a way that feels good to you week in week out. This isn't one of those books where you feel GREAT when doing it and then, a few months later, you need to pick it back up to feel those highs again; this is all about sustainable manifesting and sustainable alignment. The tools you've gained in these pages are designed to serve you in every season of your life and, most importantly, to support you moving forward. So remember that these teachings and aligned abundance will be available to you both energetically and physically in all the days to come.

How to Stay Aligned

As you enter the new seasons of your life, you will inevitably experience challenges, lessons and hurdles with your alignment. If we were in constant alignment and harmony, how would we ever learn, grow and up-level? The goal isn't to be perfect or even force alignment; it's to simply flow with the energy, opportunities and abundance presented to you in each new season of your life. You may flow with life and not need to pick up this book for years, or you may work on a new manifestation in a few months' time and want to revisit these teachings and tools to help you effortlessly manifest. There's no right or wrong here, it's your alignment journey. You may also be faced with other challenges along your path, such as feeling unregulated after a stressful period, feeling like you want to realign and unpack past emotions, feeling blocked with a new manifestation, feeling out of sorts or lost; or maybe you're reaching a new turning point in your life, such as a new decade, and want to get to know this version of yourself and work with the energy this new decade has to offer.

There are so many opportunities for you to tap back in to alignment in both small and big ways and if you encounter any of the difficulties I've just mentioned or even something that I haven't, then please know that aligned abundance will be waiting to welcome you with a warm embrace whenever you need it. No matter what challenges or unexpected situations arise in your life, know that you are divinely loved by the Universe and that this too shall pass. Don't be afraid to prioritize time for self-care, hermit yourself away or put the books down and just go live your life. Your intuition is always guiding you and you can never make a wrong decision. So keep going, and keep up the practices and rituals that set your soul on fire and align you with joy, happiness and bliss. You are the creator of your world and you're the one who decides that this journey gets to be fun, expansive and joyful.

So how are you going to maintain alignment and continue to magnetize aligned abundance to yourself? First of all, it's important to flow with the season of life that you're in and witness that everything expands and contracts, everything ebbs and flows. You're no different; so trust the cycles of your life and that everything is divinely perfect; it's exactly where your soul need to be. Continue to honour your soul and what your body needs. Listen to those nudges and niggles in your body, your nervous system and your intuition to keep the connection strong and to follow the flow of alignment in your life. Listen, too, to your feelings and emotions when they arise, listen to your soul, listen to your desires and listen to your body when it feels unregulated or needs to rest. The key to our alignment lies in our ability to listen, pause and pivot.

Remember that consistency only becomes a constant in your life if it feels fun, light and expansive. If any tools, practices or actions start to feel stagnant, it's time to switch it up. Although you may not feel high-vibe and in alignment on every single day of the year, sustainability in your vibration is maintained through consistency and energy. So if you put this book down and don't implement (or embody) its teachings, then you may notice feelings of misalignment creep back into your life. But I have full faith in you that you're not going to do that and that from here on in, you're going to prioritize your alignment and continue to create such incredible magic in your life.

One Final Aligned Action

To wrap up such powerful and potent manifestation work, in your notebook or journal I want you to write a love letter to your higher self (your future self who is in your highest timeline), detailing your commitments and intentions, moving forward. What do you promise to embody to bring your dream life into your abundant reality? What commitments and action can you take to make your aligned abundance inevitable? What intentions or manifestations are you setting for the rest of the year, now that you've a better understanding of your alignment?

Now, I don't want to direct your love letter to your future self too much, so allow yourself to flow and let the words flow through your pen or hands. Keep this letter safe and pop it in an envelope either in your manifestation box or journal, or name the file on your phone/computer "Read me in 12 months' time". Set a reminder to read your letter after 12 months. I can't wait to see what manifests for you, Queen!

Thank you for putting your trust in me with this book and for allowing me guide you to aligned abundance. Take a moment to breathe in the gratitude for yourself, for completing this book and for committing to yourself and growth – what an incredible achievement! I'm forever grateful for the opportunity to write books, as it makes my soul so happy, so thank you for always being my biggest supporters and one epic online family. The love and support you show me and others in this community always fill my heart with so much joy.

Lastly, I want you to remember this feeling of aligned abundance in your heart – the feeling of your soul, your intuition and your power. You've reclaimed your power, Queen, and that's an unstoppable magnet for abundance in this Universe! You are worthy and deserving of the most incredible joys and happiness this Universe has to offer. Get ready to welcome in your highest timeline, your dreams and alignment – it's your turn to receive your aligned abundance ...

Resources

You can find the resources, meditations and printable worksheets mentioned throughout the book at: www.emmamumford.co.uk/alignedabundance

Through this link, you'll also be able to access the bonus workshop that comes with this book, along with other extras! There's also an accompanying 11-track *Aligned Abundance* meditation playlist that can be purchased via my website shop to help take your *Aligned Abundance* journey deeper. Visit: www.emmamumford.co.uk/shop/

Other Books by the Author

Spiritual Queen (That Guy's House, 2019)
Positively Wealthy (Watkins Publishing, 2020)
Positively Wealthy Journal (Watkins Publishing, 2020)
Hurt, Healing, Healed (Watkins Publishing, 2022)
Manifesting Rituals Oracle Deck (Quercus Publishing, 2023)
Manifesting Rituals Oracle Book (Quercus, Publishing 2024)

References

Introduction

Dan Diamond, "Just 8% of People Achieve Their New Year's Resolutions. Here's How They Do It", *Forbes*, 1 Jan 2013. Available at: www.forbes.com/sites/dandiamond/2013/01/01/just-8-of-people-achieve-their-new-years-resolutions-heres-how-they-did-it/

Sakshi Sharma, "Hashtags And Influencers Have Reduced Manifestation To A Mere Trend. It's So Much More Than That", Elle India, 17 Jun. 2022. Available at: elle.in/has-manifestation-lost-its-meaning/

1. The Law of Attraction and Alignment

Brad Yates YouTube Channel. Available at: www.youtube.com/@tapwithbrad

2. Raise Your Vibration

Emma Mumford, "Raise Your Vibes and Feel Good Meditation". Available at: www.youtu.be/3sgHOZ5XeKY?

Emma Mumford, "Raise Your Vibration Subliminal". Available at: www.emmamumford.co.uk/alignedabundance alongside the books resources.

4. Manifest from a Place of Regulation

Wim Hof, "Wim Hof Method" (cold water therapy and breathwork). Available at: www.wimhofmethod.com/

Dr Bessel van der Kolk, The Body Keeps the Score: Brain, Mind, and Body in the Healing of Trauma (Penguin, 2015).

Jessica Maguire, The Nervous System Reset: Unlock the power of your vagus nerve to overcome trauma, pain and chronic stress (Bluebird, 2024).

Emma Mumford, "Align Your Energy and Chakras Meditation". Available at: www.youtu.be/Y3RTYGua3Nc?

5. Declutter Your Energy and Life

HIPPO survey quoted in Pier Marketing, 56% of Brits Admit to Clutter Chaos, Response resource website, 28 Mar. 2022. Available at: www.pressreleases.responsesource.com/news/102511/56-of-brits-admit-to-clutter-chaos/

Marie Kondo, The Life-Changing Magic of Tidying: A simple, effective way to banish clutter forever (Vermilion, 2014).

National Soap Association survey quoted in Kelly McMenamin, "Why Decluttering Is Hard: Retailers' use of consumer psychology makes it tough to let go", Psychology Today website, 17 Feb.

2022. Available at: www.psychologytoday.com/gb/blog/natural-order/202202/why-decluttering-is-hard

6. Release Expectations and Control

Emma Mumford, "Releasing Expectations and Control Meditation". Available at: www.emmamumford.co.uk/alignedabundance alongside the books resources.

7. Get to Know Your Authentic Self

Emma Mumford, "Embodying Self-Worth". Available at: www.youtu.be/8lTqUSFnCoQ?
Emma Mumford, "Releasing Old Identities and Cord Cutting Meditation". Available via the author's website in the *Aligned Abundance* meditation playlist. You can purchase the complete meditation playlist at: www.emmamumford.co.uk/alignedabundance

9. Alignment versus Divine Timing

Alaistair Gunn, "The Earth's rotation is changing speed: should we be worried?", *Science Focus*, website (n.d). Available at: www.sciencefocus.com/planet-earth/earth-rotation-speed

11. Live with Intention

Marie Forleo, Time Genius®. For more information, visit: www.marieforleo.com/time-genius

12. Manifest with Joy

Emma Mumford, "Spiritual Queen's Vibe Raising Playlist", Spotify playlist. Available at www.emmamumford.uk/3JH2yzp
Emma Mumford, "Core Energy of your Desire Mediation". Available at: www.emmamumford.co.uk/alignedabundance and www.emmamumford.uk/coreenergy

14. Flow, Don't Force

Emma Mumford, "Flow, Release and Surrender Meditation". Available via the author's website in the *Aligned Abundance* meditation playlist. You can purchase the complete meditation playlist at: www.emmamumford.co.uk/alignedabundance

Acknowledgements

As I sit here at the end of a nine-month journey with this book, I can't help but feel in awe at the magic and magnetism within these pages. Although I'm the one who writes the book, I never know how it will flow or what it will transform into, until I take step back at the end and read the words my soul has poured onto the pages. This has absolutely been the most enjoyable book for me to write so far and it came through thick and fast, which has been both an expansive and joyous journey for me. I feel so honoured that I get to birth *Aligned Abundance* into the world and that I get to be your guide on this journey. Thank you from the bottom of my heart for allowing me to write these wonderful books for you and remind you of your innate power and magic. I love each and every one of you!

Of course, I couldn't make this journey alone and I want to take this opportunity to express my gratitude to my nearest and dearest for their endless support, patience and love during the book-writing process. Nine months has been my shortest deadline to date for writing a book, so I've been hidden away with my laptop most of the year and spending most weekends writing with Luna napping by my side. Thank you as always to my Happy Mermaids for your endless support, advice and for being the most incredible friends: I love you both dearly. Thank you to Hannah for always believing in me, holding me and this year walking me down the aisle too! Thank you to Alex, my incredible fiancé, and Luna the bestest Dachshund for being my aligned abundance in life: I will never know how I got so lucky with you both and you two are my biggest muses in life and work. Thank you for the endless cups of tea during writing and your support and encouragement during this process. I also can't forget my beloved grandad who left this Earth halfway through my writing this book; since your passing so much transformation and alignment has happened in my life and I know you'll be looking down on me now so proud that I've released another book into the world. Thank you for always believing in me and for being the best grandad I could have asked for.

I also want to express deep gratitude to my team for creating the space for me to write this book: Leanne, you are a true superstar – thank you for your endless support, love and wisdom, I am so proud to have you on the team. Celina, our number one hype woman, thank you for always hyping me and our wonderful community. And thank you to Amy and Mischa, too, for sharing your wonderful energy in the world and in my business. I'm so lucky to have the most incredible women on my team who inspire me daily. And of course the wonderful team at Watkins – thank you, Fiona, for once again believing in my work, and Laura, Monica, Brittany and Christiana for making this work a dream and for being the best publishing team, full of positivity, support and love. Finally, to Sue, my incredible editor who without fail turns my words into the magical books you read – her ability to see the potential in these manuscripts and turn them into the most flowing, aligned masterpieces never ceases to amaze me. Thank you all for supporting me and this book in moments of doubt, wobble and tight deadlines. I feel honoured and proud to have the best team around me who are all so inspiring. Although my original commissioning editor, Anya, has left Watkins now, I want to thank you also for always championing my work and for making my journey as an author possible.

Last but certainly not least, I want to thank you, my incredible readers and community! Without you none of this would be possible and this book is from my heart to yours. Thank you for supporting me, trusting in my work and for being the kindest souls. Every time I have the joy of interacting with you, whether it's in my online containers or even in person, I'm blown away by just how kind, positive and lovely you all are. It's an honour having you here and being your guide. I feel so lucky to be able to witness all of your beautiful transformations daily. Thank you also to my awesome clients and Membership Queens who allowed me to share their stories in this book. Every day, I wake up and feel incredibly lucky to do what I do for a living and you all make it so special and magical every day – thank you, thank you, thank you.

About the Author

Emma Mumford is the UK's leading Law of Attraction expert. She is an award-winning life coach, 3x bestselling author of *Positively Wealthy*, *Hurt, Healing, Healed* and *Manifesting Rituals*, Law of Attraction YouTuber, speaker and host of the popular podcast "Spiritual Queen's Badass Podcast". Emma's work helps people turn their dream life into an abundant reality using the Law of Attraction and spirituality. Through her work, Emma has helped hundreds of thousands of people globally over the last decade.

Emma started her money-saving journey to abundance back in 2013. After finding couponing in her hour of need – thanks to her ex-boyfriend leaving her with his £7,000 debt – Emma then set up the nationally popular brand Extreme Couponing and Deals UK and became known as the UK's Coupon Queen. In 2016, Emma underwent a spiritual awakening and knew that her calling in life was to move away from her money-saving roots and grow into the personal development world with her own brand. Emma has since sold her first business and now focuses on her spiritual work full-time.

www.emmamumford.co.uk | @iamemmamumford

WATKINS
1893

The story of Watkins began in 1893, when scholar of esotericism John Watkins founded our bookshop, inspired by the lament of his friend and teacher Madame Blavatsky that there was nowhere in London to buy books on mysticism, occultism or metaphysics. That moment marked the birth of Watkins, soon to become the publisher of many of the leading lights of spiritual literature, including Carl Jung, Rudolf Steiner, Alice Bailey and Chögyam Trungpa.

Today, the passion at Watkins Publishing for vigorous questioning is still resolute. Our stimulating and groundbreaking list ranges from ancient traditions and complementary medicine to the latest ideas about personal development, holistic wellbeing and consciousness exploration. We remain at the cutting edge, committed to publishing books that change lives.

DISCOVER MORE AT:
www.watkinspublishing.com

Read our blog

Watch and listen to
our authors in action

Sign up to
our mailing list

We celebrate conscious, passionate, wise and happy living.
Be part of that community by visiting

 /watkinspublishing  @watkinswisdom
/watkinsbooks  @watkinswisdom